Conversations with Ernest Hemingway

Literary Conversations Series

Peggy Whitman Prenshaw
General Editor

Conversations with Ernest Hemingway

Edited by
Matthew J. Bruccoli

University Press of Mississippi
Jackson and London

Books by Ernest Hemingway

Three Stories and Ten Poems. Paris: Contact Publishing Co., 1923.
in our time. Paris: Three Mountains Press, 1924.
In Our Time. New York: Boni & Liveright, 1925.
The Torrents of Spring. New York: Charles Scribner's Sons, 1926.
The Sun Also Rises. New York: Charles Scribner's Sons, 1926.
Men Without Women. New York: Charles Scribner's Sons, 1927.
A Farewell to Arms. New York: Charles Scribner's Sons, 1929.
Death in the Afternoon. New York: Charles Scribner's Sons, 1932.
Winner Take Nothing. New York: Charles Scribner's Sons, 1933.
Green Hills of Africa. New York: Charles Scribner's Sons, 1935.
To Have and Have Not. New York: Charles Scribner's Sons, 1937.
The Fifth Column and the First Forty-nine Stories. New York: Charles Scribner's Sons, 1938.
For Whom the Bell Tolls. New York: Charles Scribner's Sons, 1940.
Across the River and into the Trees. New York: Charles Scribner's Sons, 1950.
The Old Man and the Sea. New York: Charles Scribner's Sons, 1952.
A Moveable Feast. New York: Charles Scribner's Sons, 1964.
Islands in the Stream. New York: Charles Scribner's Sons, 1970.
The Dangerous Summer. New York: Charles Scribner's Sons, 1985.

Library of Congress Cataloging-in-Publication Data
Conversations with Ernest Hemingway.

(Literary conservations series)
Includes index.
1. Hemingway, Ernest, 1899–1961—Interviews.
2. Authors, American—20th century—Interviews.
I. Bruccoli, Matthew Joseph, 1931–   II. Series.
PS3515.E37Z58467 1986   813'.52   86-11140
ISBN 0-87805-272-0
ISBN 0-87805-273-9 (pbk.)

Contents

Introduction

It is not *un-natural* that the best writers are liars. A major part of their trade is to lie or invent and they will lie when they are drunk, or to themselves, or to strangers. They often lie unconsciously and then remember their lies with deep remorse. If they knew all other writers were liars too it would cheer them up.[1]

Late one August night in 1952 I noticed a small crowd around a Times Square newsstand where the next day's new magazines were being put out. The people were waiting to buy the *Life* issue with *The Old Man and the Sea*—which sold out 5,300,000 copies in two days. Charles Dickens's readers are reported to have lined up all night to obtain the installments of his novels; but Ernest Hemingway was the only American writer who could have generated the scene I observed. It didn't matter that *The Old Man and the Sea* is a minor work. Hemingway was making a comeback—or defending his title, as he put it—and that did matter because he was important to many kinds of people for many reasons. In certain ways Hemingway overshadowed his work.

Hemingway was the most recognizable writer of the twentieth century—indeed, the best-known American writer of all time. It has been twenty-five years since his suicide, but he doesn't seem dead at all. John O'Hara may have been correct in designating Hemingway the most important writer since the death of Shakespeare. People who had never read his books—or any book—recognized his photo and his name. Yet he was much more than a media celebrity. His personal fame and his literary reputation coalesced into a legendary—or mythical—figure who represented American literature in his time. Everything Hemingway did seemed to have something to do with literature: hunting, fishing, boozing, brawling, warring, wiving.

1. Kennedy Library. Quoted in Michael S. Reynolds, *Hemingway's Reading 1910–1940* (Princeton: Princeton University Press, 1981), p. 4.

Who else could have compelled Americans to regard the bullfight as material for literature?

His fame was not accidentally acquired. Hemingway's greatest character was Ernest Hemingway. From boyhood he assiduously fictionalized himself. He was a dedicated careerist who skillfully nurtured an heroic public image until the vainglorious role took over the man and it became necessary for him to live up to it. The public Papa and the private writer were eventually undifferentiable. His impersonation of Ernest Hemingway was so successful because he was having such a good time at it. The Hemingway who emerges from these reports is a man living life to the hilt—deriving maximum value from experience—while achieving lasting work. Perhaps one of the reasons for the attraction he exerted is that he was a wish-fulfiller. Those who read about him or heard about him participated in the vicarious enjoyment of being Hemingway.

Along with his exhibitionism and bragging, Hemingway was always a spokesman for literature. He talked about writing with the authority of a master and always delivered the message that great writing was the most important thing in the world: "A country, finally, erodes and the dust blows away, the people all die and none of them were of any importance permanently, except those who practised the arts. . . ."[2] Hemingway was not just an influence on other writers; he made literature important to people who did not earn their livings—directly or indirectly—from it. His insistence on the element of competition in his own work enhanced the importance of literature for outsiders who regarded writing as a precious avocation. He meant it when he boasted that "I started out very quiet and I beat Mr. Turgenev. Then I trained very hard and I beat Mr. de Maupassant. I've fought two draws with Mr. Stendhal, and I think I had an edge in the last one. But nobody's going to get me in the ring with Mr. Tolstoy unless I'm crazy or I keep getting better."[3]

Hemingway's strenuous life provided good newspaper copy, and he appropriately lived to read his own obituaries after the 1954 African plane crashes. Although he complained about interruptions and invasions of his privacy, he was accessible to journalists, who were accorded the full Hemingway treatment. On his visits to New

2. *Green Hills of Africa* (New York: Scribner's, 1935).

3. Lillian Ross, "How Do You Like it Now, Gentlemen?" *New Yorker,* 26 (13 May 1950), 36–62.

York he palled around with syndicated gossip columnists. Even seasoned celebrity-hunters responded to the Hemingway charm and force of personality. While openly contemptuous of what he called the critical "angle worms," Hemingway was careful to keep his activities in the literary news; Harvey Breit of the *New York Times Book Review* served as a reliable messenger.

Most of Hemingway's career came before the period of the in-depth interview or conversation. The 1950 *New Yorker* profile by Lillian Ross presented an absurd Hemingway; thereafter he avoided extended, formal interviews, informing his old friend Chink Dorman-O'Gowan:

> I am as sick of Profiles as of the palsy. What can you tell them? . . . They can't read a map and who gives them the co-ordinates on where your heart is located and when they have the coordinates it means nothing. . . .
> Who wants to speak about injustice; who wants to make a spiel on sorrow? Who wants to sound off on how his father killed himself or how his mother robbed him of his inheritance? Byron maybe; not me. I just want to talk quietly on the telephone, understand the map, throw in the counter attack where it should go exactly on time and go to hell and meet nice people.[4]

Prior to the fifties he was mainly represented through shipboard or airport interviews when going to or coming from a war or an adventure. The only extended Hemingway literary interview, the 1958 *Paris Review* "Writers at Work" document, is not a conversation at all—consisting of his written replies to written questions. It has been necessary to augment the straight interviews in this volume with Hemingway's public statements, which contributed to the formation of his persona. The only speech he delivered—at the 1937 American Writers' Congress—and his Nobel Prize acceptance statement are included in an appendix.

The documents assembled here are sometimes contradictory, but it is impossible to determine in *every* case whether Hemingway or the reporter was to blame.[5] Despite his proclaimed reliance on a "built-in, shock-proof, shit detector," he was not compulsively truthful—as

---

4. To General E. E. Dorman-O'Gowan, lot # 167, *English Literature and History* (London: Sotheby's, 1985).

5. The interviews are reprinted here as they originally appeared—without emendations, except for regularization of book and story titles. The publisher styled the headlines and eliminated the subheads.

his deceptions about completed novels in the bank reveal. Still, his lies were part of the Hemingway mechanism.

Those of us who grew up with the face of Ernest Hemingway on the covers of mass-circulation magazines feel a vacancy. While aggrandizing himself, he aggrandized the practice of reading and writing.

MJB
March 1986

Chronology

1899	21 July, birth, in Oak Park, Illinois
1918	8 July, wounding in Italy
1921	3 September, marriage to Hadley Richardson
1923	Publication of *Three Stories & Ten Poems*
1924	Publication of *in our time*
1925	Publication of *In Our Time*
1926	Publication of *The Sun Also Rises*
1927	Publication of *Men Without Women*
1927	10 May, marriage to Pauline Pfeiffer
1929	Publication of *A Farewell to Arms*
1932	Publication of *Death in the Afternoon*
1933	Publication of *Winner Take Nothing*
1935	Publication of *Green Hills of Africa*
1936–39	Spanish Civil War
1937	Publication of *To Have and Have Not*
1940	21 November, marriage to Martha Gellhorn

Conversations with Ernest Hemingway

Has 227 Wounds, but Is Looking for Job
New York Sun/1919

Reprinted from the *New York Sun* (22 January 1919), 8.

The first wounded American from the Italian front arrived yesterday by the steamship Giuseppe Verdi of the Transatlantica Italiano line with probably more scars than any other man in or out of uniform, who defied the shrapnel of the Central Powers.

His wounds might have been much less if he had not been constructed by nature on generous proportions, being more than six feet tall and of ample beam.

He is Ernest M. Hemingway, before the war a reporter for the *Kansas City Star,* and hailing from Oak Park, Ill. The surgical chart of his battered person shows 227 marks, indicating where bits of a peculiar kind of Austrian shrapnel, about as thick as a .22 calibre bullet and an inch long, like small cuts from a length of wire, smote him. Some of these bits have been extracted after a dozen or more operations and young Hemingway hopes finally to get them all out, but he still retains a hundred or more.

Hemingway joined the Red Cross in France and was transferred to the Italian front last July. He was distributing cigarettes in the Piave district in the front line trenches when a shell from a trench mortar burst over his head. He said the slugs from the shell felt like the stings of wasps as they bore into him. He crumpled up and two Italian stretcher bearers started over the parapet with him, knowing that he needed swift attention. Austrian machine gunners spotted the party and before they could get over he and the stretcher bearers went down under a storm of machine gun bullets, one of which got Hemingway in the shoulder and another in the right leg. Two of his stretcher men took the tall American through the communication trenches in the rear, where he received first aid.

Hemingway was in the Red Cross Hospital at Milan three months and the surgeons extracted thirty-two fragments from his head and body, telling him he was in for a series of operations that might last a

1

year or more. He is preparing for such an ordeal, which he hopes will relieve some of his lameness. After that he believes he will be qualified to take a job on any New York newspaper that wants a man that is not afraid of work and wounds.

He did not give up war work when he got rid of those thirty-two slugs. Weary of doing nothing, he obtained permission to go to the front again in October, staying there until the armistice.

Hemingway Speaks to High School
Edwin Wells/1919

Reprinted from the Oak Park High School *Trapeze* (21 March 1919), 1, 3.

Lieut. Ernest M. Hemingway, '17, late of the Italian Ambulance Service of the American Red Cross and then of the Italian Army spoke of his experiences in Italy at assembly last Friday. Caroline Bagley a classmate of the speaker introduced him to an audience the greater part of which already knew him.

"Stein" as he has been nicknamed, had lost none of the manner of speech which made his Ring Lardner letters for the *Trapeze* of several years ago so interesting. He told of his experiences first in a quiet sector in the Lower Piave and last in the final big Italian drive.

He seemed especially interested in a division of the Italian Army called "Arditi." "These men" he said, "had been confined in the Italian penal institutions, having committed some slight mistake such as—well—murder or arson, and were released on the condition that they would serve in this division which was used by the government for shock troops.

Armed only with revolvers, hand grenades, and two bladed short swords, they attacked, frequently stripped to the waist. Their customary loss in an engagement was about two-thirds."

On the day of which Lieut. Hemingway was speaking, they came up in camions, the whole regiment singing a song which from any other body of men would have meant three months in jail. Hemingway sang the song for the audience in Italian and then translated it. Several hours after their initial engagement with the enemy, Lieutenant Hemingway saw a wounded captain being brought back to a field hospital in an ambulance.

He had been shot in the chest but had plugged the holes with cigarettes and gone on fighting. On his way to the hospital he amused himself by throwing hand grenades into the ditch just to see them go off. This illustrates the spirit of these men.

At the time he was wounded Lieut. Hemingway was assigned to the 69th Regiment of Infantry. He was with several Italians in an advanced listening post. It was at night but the enemy had probably noticed them, for he dropped a trench mortar shell, which consists of a gallon can filled with explosive and slugs, into the hole in which they were.

"When the thing exploded," Lieut. Hemingway said, "it seemed as if I was moving off somewhere in a sort of red din. I said to myself, 'Gee! Stein, you're dead' and then I began to feel myself pulling back to earth. Then I woke up. The sand bags had caved in on my legs and at first I felt disappointed that I had not been wounded. The other soldiers had retreated leaving me and several others for dead. One of these soldiers who was left started crying. So I knew he was alive and told him to shut up. The Austrians seemed determined to wipe out this one outpost. They had star shells out and their trench searchlights were trying to locate us.

"I picked up the wounded man and started back toward the trenches. As I got up to walk my knee cap felt warm and sticky, so I knew I'd been touched. Just before we reached the trench their searchlight spotted us and they turned a machine gun on us. One got me in the thigh. It felt just like a snowball, so hard and coming with such force that it knocked me down. We started on, but just as we reached the trench and were about to jump in, another bullet hit me, this time in the foot. It tumbled me and my wounded man all in a heap in the trench and when I came to again I was in a dugout. Two soldiers had just come to the conclusion that I was to 'pass out shortly.' By some arguing I was able to convince them they were wrong."

So Lieut. Hemingway told his modest story of the incident for which he was awarded the highest decoration given by the Italian Government. In addition to his medals, one of which was conferred personally by the King of Italy, Lieut. Hemingway has a captured Austrian automatic revolver, a gas mask and his punctured trousers. Besides these trophies he has his field equipment which he wore into the assembly hall.

While in Oak Park High he was prominent in the school's activities. He was on *The Trapeze* staff for two years and was one of the editors in his last year. Always interested in athletics, he won his monogram in football and was manager of the track team.*

*Students were asked to learn this song for the assembly at which Hemingway spoke:

> Hemingway, we hail you the victor,
> Hemingway, ever winning the game,
> Hemingway, you've carried the colors
> For our land you've won fame.
> Hemingway, we hail you the leader,
> Your deeds—every one shows your valor.
> Hemingway, Hemingway, you've won
> —Hemingway!

Trapeze (14 March 1919), 1—MJB.

Stalking Lions Was "Exciting" to Hemingway

New York Herald Tribune/1934

Reprinted from the *New York Herald Tribune* (4 April 1934), 4.
© I.H.T. Corporation. Reprinted by permission.

Ernest Hemingway, enthusiastic over the three months he had passed
in East Africa stalking big game with rifle and camera, returned
yesterday on the French liner Paris with Mrs. Hemingway, who
shared his adventures. Mr. Hemingway was in such high spirits that
he granted an interview, something unusual for him.

"It's hard to describe just what there is to killing big game," he told
the shipnews reporters. "It's very exciting and—uh—it gives you a
fine feeling. It's the sort of the same thing as any killing; that is, it's
fine if you do a clean job of it and it's lousy if there's bad
sportsmanship."

Expanding on the sporting angle, Mr. Hemingway said that he shot
only lions that were utter strangers to him; the animals that he had
had trailed for photographs he could not bring himself to kill.

"It's something like writing the truth about people on an island," he
observed. "You can do one book on the subject, but after a while
you get to know and like almost everybody, then you're through as
far as writing about them is concerned."

Mr. Hemingway had the good fortune to see a total of ninety-six
lions during his hunt, and he obtained photographs of twenty-nine
lionesses "preening themselves like a group of finishing school girls."

Comparing the killing qualities of African game, Mr. Hemingway
gave first honors to the leopards "because they strike the fastest."
The lion was ranked next, Mr. Hemingway having timed one and
found it could cover 100 yards in three seconds when about to kill.
The Cape buffalo "can take the most punishment but is dumb" and
is treacherous when wounded, according to Mr. Hemingway, who
told how one of these beasts was wounded and lost itself in the

bushes, only to charge on the Hemingway party. The author shot it at a distance of fifteen yards.

Mr. Hemingway trailed lions which themselves were trailing a herd of wildebeests estimated at 3,000,000 by the Kenya Colony Game Department. The wildebeests were following the rains in unprecedented numbers, because of the drought in East Africa.

He brought back some superb photographs of lions making their kills, but does not intend to publish those until he can spend a year or so in Africa. He believes that much time will be required to learn "anything worth writing about." He did not think there was much danger to big game hunting, except that the hunter likes to get a closer range each time be shoots, and this makes for unfortunate contacts with fast beasts who move toward and not away.

Mr. and Mrs. Hemingway had been abroad for eight months, three of which were spent in Africa. Mr. Hemingway admitted that a surfeit of the formalized spectacle of bullfighting such as he depicted in his *Death in the Afternoon* was responsible for his reversion to hunting, the sport of his teens.

The pursuit of game having renewed his enthusiasm for life, he returned home "to work like hell and make enough money so that I can go back to Africa and really learn something about lions." He is completing a novel and will work on it at his home in Key West.

As for authors, he discussed various writers at length, but strictly off the record.

Hemingway Sees Defeat of Franco

New York Times/1937

Reprinted from the *New York Times* (19 May 1937), 10. Copyright © 1937 by The New York Times Company. Reprinted by permission.

Ernest Hemingway, novelist and war correspondent, returned from Spain yesterday on the French liner Normandie after spending several weeks with the Loyalist forces on the Madrid front.

Mr. Hemingway said it was his conviction that the Insurgents were doomed to defeat, because he considered Madrid an impregnable city favored with natural defense possibilities which General Franco could never overcome. He pictured the Loyalists as growing stronger every day in forces and morale, and the insurgents growing weaker.

"The reason why Franco is out of luck," Mr. Hemingway said, "is that Madrid lies in this big plateau, with all the defensive forces grouped together and fighting from the inside, like a boxer; they can make Franco lead every time anywhere along his tremendous front. To do so he has to move many times as far as the defenders. And each time there they are, waiting for him.

He said the Spanish civil war had undoubtedly delayed "the coming European war" for years, because it has served as a proving ground for European war machinery. For one thing it had demonstrated that the German equipment is not up to what it should be for continental warfare, he declared.

The author said that Spain revisited was a revelation to him. He expected to encounter great difficulty getting to Madrid, but had none. In sections of the country where fighting is not being waged he found the people living normally, going ahead with their farming as though the rest of the country were not inflamed by war. He said he expected to find most of his old Madrid friends killed, but he found all but two or three still living in Madrid, unharmed.

"If General Franco takes Bilbao the war will probably continue for another two years, and if he doesn't the war could possibly end late

this Fall or in the Spring," he said. "The war has changed greatly. It is
no longer a war of militia, but a serious war of trained troops, and the
forces of the defenders of Madrid increase their strength every week,
and time is definitely on their side. Franco has been hammering away
at Madrid since last November, and he lost his chance to take the city
in that first month."

He said General Franco's Moorish troops had been largely "killed
off" and that there were no more to be had. Another arm of the
insurgent force from which much was expected, the Italian division,
suffered complete rout before the Loyalists, and the Italians have
demonstrated their complete inability to fight on foreign soil, "at least
not in Spain," Mr. Hemingway declared.

He said the Italians lost more men at Brihuega than in the entire
Ethiopian compaign.

As to the German factor in the war, the author said that as far as he
could find out there was no German infantry serving with General
Franco, all the German soldiers being in the artillery, the air force,
transport, signal corps, anti-aircraft and tank corps or serving as
technicians.

Hemingway Links Fate
of Democracy with Spain

Los Angeles Times/1937

Reprinted from the *Los Angeles Times* (12 July 1937), 3.
Copyright, 1937, *Los Angeles Times*. Reprinted by permission.

The fate of Spain is the fate of that part of the world believing in the democratic form of government.

This was the conviction expressed yesterday at the Hollywood Plaza by Ernest Hemingway, novelist and correspondent just back from four months with the loyalist armies.

As a correspondent, Hemingway covered the loyalist front for months, carried camera equipment for Photographer Joris Ivens during the precarious filming of *Spanish Earth,* first record of the civil war.

The picture, for which Hemingway wrote the narrative, will be shown at the Philharmonic Auditorium tomorrow at 8:30 p.m. for the benefit of the Spanish ambulance corps which the author and John Dos Passos helped organize.

The writer sees eventual success for the loyalists, unless Italy throws in her entire army on behalf of the rebels. For he feels that the dominant sentiment in Spain today is in support of the Madrid government.

"There probably won't be any European war for at least a year," he explained. "Perhaps never. Spain is the gymnasium training essential to a fighter before he actually enters the ring. And such nations as Italy have had nasty shocks."

Tales of executions by the loyalists are untrue, he added. During his stay in Madrid he saw prisoners brought in and placed in prison camps. He talked with them, thus ascertaining the numbers of foreign troops on Spanish soil.

"I know nothing of what happens in the camps of the rebels," he said. "My only knowledge is what I actually saw with the government troops."

The number of Russians actually taking part in the Spanish war is small, according to Hemingway. In his fifty-four days at the front, he saw no more than sixty Russians. Food has been sent by the soviets to the loyalists, while supplies all have been paid for by the government.

Women soldiers today are few, he said. In the early days of the war, many women enlisted but proved a source of grave difficulty.

Fried in Florida, Stewed in N.Y., but in S.F.—Ah!

San Francisco Chronicle/1937

Ernest Hemingway, one of the brilliant young novelists produced by post-war America, arrived in San Francisco yesterday "to get cool."

On his first visit to San Francisco, he gulped in a few cubic yards of fog shortly after stepping from a United Air Lines plane at the San Francisco Airport and sighed:

"Say, this is great! After frying in New York, stewing down in Florida and sweltering in Los Angeles this is something like summer weather. I can't for the life of me see why anybody would ever move out of San Francisco, particularly in the summer time."

The novelist, who has now turned war correspondent with the Spanish loyalist forces, flew here from Los Angeles. He is accompanied by his wife with whom, he explained, he is trying to become acquainted after months in war-torn Spain.

He came to the film capital from his home in Bimini, Fla. to act as narrator and scenarist for *The Spanish Earth,* a motion picture which gives the visual story of the Spanish revolution from the loyalist side of the lines.

"There is plenty of action in that picture," he volunteered. "I know it because I carried the camera.

"To get some of our shots we went into actual battle inside tanks. Beside us marched the loyalist infantry, and we shot their faces as they marched toward the enemy. That is the kind of realism Hollywood can't touch."

With him came Joris Ivens, young Dutch motion picture director, who supervised the filming of the battle scenes.

Hemingway is not in the least bit like the man one might picture him after reading *Death in the Afternoon, A Farewell to Arms, Men*

Without Women,The Sun Also Rises, In Our Time. Although from
these books one would scarcely picture their author as a Michael
Arlen or a Noel Coward, you might expect to find a sophisticated,
suave sort of William Powell.

Instead, he is a big hulk of a man, well over 6 feet and with the
shoulders of a fullback, with dark, wavy hair and a round quick-to-
smile face. About him is a certain air of shyness, a rather boyish
quality that appears to deprecate any attempt at lionizing, to laugh off
any attempt to make him a hero, a world figure.

He looks the type of man who would be far more at home in a
small boat battling a giant swordfish than in a drawing room, much
more at ease with a rifle in his hand than a teacup. As indeed he is.

"Thanks be for a few quiet days of vacation and rest in this blessed
cool weather," he breathed. "Then back to Florida and my kids and
my boat, and then back to Spain some time in August.

There's plenty of work to be done there yet."

Hemingway Slaps Eastman in Face

New York Times/1937

Reprinted from the *New York Times* (14 August 1937), 15. Copyright © 1937 by The New York Times Company. Reprinted by permission.

Ernest Hemingway says he slapped Max Eastman's face with a book in the offices of Charles Scribner's Sons, publishers, and Max Eastman says he then threw Hemingway over a desk and stood him on his head in a corner.

They both tell of the face-slapping, but Mr. Hemingway denies Mr. Eastman threw him anywhere or stood him on his head in any place, and says that he will donate $1,000 to any charity Mr. Eastman may name—or even to Mr. Eastman himself—for the pleasure of Mr. Eastman's company in a locked room with all legal rights waived.

Mr. Eastman's most recent book was *The Enjoyment of Laughter,* published by Simon & Schuster.

He was sitting in Max Perkins's office at Scribner's Wednesday—Mr. Perkins is editor for that firm—discussing a new book called *The Enjoyment of Poetry,* when Mr. Hemingway walked in, he said yesterday.

Using a few *Death in the Afternoon* phrases in what he describes as a "kidding manner," Mr. Hemingway commented on an essay by Mr. Eastman that had been entitled "Bull in the Afternoon."

Mr. Eastman had written:

"Come out from behind that false hair on your chest, Ernest. We all know you."

The volume containing this essay happened to be on Mr. Perkins's crowded desk, "and when I saw that," says Mr. Hemingway, "I began to get sore."

In what he hoped was a playful manner, he said, he bared his chest to Mr. Eastman and asked him to look at the hair and say whether it was false.

He persuaded Mr. Eastman to bare his chest and commented on its comparatively hairless condition.

"We were just fooling around, in a way," Mr. Hemingway said yesterday. "But when I looked at him and I thought about the book, I got sore. I tried to get him to read to me, in person, some of the stuff he had written about me. He wouldn't do it. So that's when I socked him with the book."

"Was he in a chair or standing up?"

"He was standing over there," pointing to a window with a window seat in Mr. Perkins's office. "I didn't really sock him. If I had I might have knocked him through that window and out into Fifth Avenue. That would be fine, wouldn't it? That would have got me in wrong with my boss, and he might have had me arrested. So, though I was sore, I just slapped him. That knocked him down. He fell back there on the window seat."

"But how about throwing you over the desk?" Mr. Hemingway was asked, "and standing you on your head in a corner?"

"He didn't throw anybody anywhere. He jumped at me like a woman—clawing, you know, with his open hands. I just held him off. I didn't want to hurt him. He's ten years older than I am."

Mr. Perkins's office retains the somewhat Old World atmosphere that it had in the days—not long past—when it was the rule that gentlemen should not smoke in Scribner's because women were employed in the offices.

"How about books and papers being knocked off the desk?" Mr. Hemingway was asked. "Mr. Eastman says—"

"Sure, some books were knocked off. He jumped at me, I held him off, there was a little, a little wrestle."

According to the Eastman version, after Mr. Hemingway was knocked down he patted Mr. Eastman's shoulder in an embarrassed fashion and smiled.

Mr. Hemingway explained that he had felt sorry for Mr. Eastman, for he knew that he had seriously embarrassed him by slapping his face.

"The man didn't have a bit of fight. He just croaked, you know, at Max Perkins. 'Who's calling on you? Ernest or me?' So I got out. But he didn't do any throwing around. He just sat and took it.

"I felt sorry for him. Max Perkins told me, he said 'no one has any right to humiliate a man the way you have.' And I guess he's right. I feel kind of sorry, but he shouldn't go around telling these lies."

Mr. Hemingway had a large swelling over his left eye, high up on his forehead. Asked if this was a result of the battle of Thursday he grinned and shook his head.

He pulled off his coat and showed a deep scar in the biceps of his right arm.

"Max Eastman didn't do that to me, either," he said. He showed another scar. "Or that."

Mr. Hemingway gave his present weight at a little under 200 pounds, said that Mr. Eastman was narrower at the shoulders, just as big around the waist.

"Here's a statement," he offered, as the interview closed. "If Mr. Eastman takes his prowess seriously—if he has not, as it seems, gone in for fiction—then let him waive all medical rights and legal claims to damages, and I'll put up $1,000 for any charity he favors or for himself. Then we'll go into a room and he can read his book to me— the part of his book about me. Well, the best man unlocks the door."

Mr. Hemingway is sailing for Spain today. It is understood that Mr. Eastman left yesterday to spend a week-end at Martha's Vineyard.

Mr. Perkins and other members of the Scribner staff refused to do more than verify the fact that the affair had taken place, taking the stand that "this is a personal matter between the two gentlemen in question."

Ernest Hemingway Talks Of Work and War

Robert Van Gelder/1940

Reprinted from the *New York Times* (11 August 1940), 2.
Copyright © 1940 by The New York Times Company. Reprinted
by permission.

Ernest Hemingway was here in New York copyreading and delivering
to Scribners, his publishers, at the rate of 300 pages a day, the final
draft of his longest novel. People who have read the manuscript agree
that it is his best. Said one such reader encountered as he waited,
rather bemused, for a chance to cross a cross-street on which there
was no traffic, one afternoon some months ago: "I've just read the
first three-quarters of the new Hemingway and you might as well
believe me because you're going to find out that it's true—it is even
better than *Farewell to Arms.*"

Mr. Hemingway's stay here was supposed to be all for work, but
cheerfulness kept breaking in. On the eleventh day of July's heat
wave his rooms at the Hotel Barclay saw as lively company as any
rooms in town. An electric fan droned on the coffee table, flanked by
bottles of White Rock and fronted by a superb bowl of ice. A fifth of
Scotch rested hospitably on the floor where it could be handily
reached from three of the four chairs. Lawyers, old friends and
visiting soldiers came and went. The telephone rang not quite
continuously. Mr. Hemingway wore an unbuttoned pajama coat
affording a view of chest that—if Max Eastman still is interested—
would have made the eyes of a fur trapper pop.

"I've worked at it solid for seventeen months," said Hemingway of
his new novel. "This one had to be all right or I had to get out of line,
because my last job, *To Have and Have Not,* was not so good. For
seventeen months I wrote no short stories or articles—nothing to earn
a penny. I'm broke."

A friend said: "Ernest, if I am paid $200 for the job I am doing
tonight we will have a wonderful time tomorrow." "Don't worry

17

about $200," said Hemingway. "Whether you get it or I get it we'll
still have a wonderful time tomorrow. Charley Scribner isn't broke."

The talk was a mixture of Spanish, French and English. Each
comment that Hemingway made on his writing he prefaced with an
explanatory speech to Gustavo Duran, the former pianist and com-
poser, who had developed as one of the most brilliant of the army
corps commanders on the Loyalist side of the civil war in Spain.

"Sorry, Gustavo, but Bob has to ask these question, it's his job,
and I'm supposed to answer them, see?" And then, rapidly: "I start
work each morning at 7:30 and work until about 2:30. The first thing
I do when I'm writing a novel is read back through all that has gone
before. That way I break the back of the job. Then I put the words
in—like laying bricks. I write in longhand and don't try to make much
time. I've tried this speed writing, getting it all down and then going
over it, but the trouble is if you speed too much you don't know if
you have a book or not when you've finished the first draft."

"About how many words do you write each day?" Duran asked,
seriously. Hemingway looked at him, not sure whether or not he was
being ribbed. "I don't know, Gustavo. Some days a lot, some days a
little. I never write to fit a thesis or a plan. I start with blank paper and
put all that I know at the time on the paper. Most of the time it is
tough going. You can't figure any average. Why in hell do you want
to know, Gustavo?"

Duran shrugged: "I don't know. It is interesting." He talked of his
own job as a commander. He said that in his army regulations the
first sentence was the seemingly meaningless one that roughly
translated into "the first duty of the commander is to make decisions."

"It seems simple when you read it. You think, 'What is decision?
Each day I decide what color shoes to wear, what to eat.' But
decision, when the life or death of hundreds of men depend on your
decision, that is much else. In Spain I was assigned, as you know, to
hold a position. My cowardice told me to draw in my left flank so that
if I failed I would be near the French border and the lives of
thousands would be saved if we lost. My judgment said perhaps that
is right but perhaps it would be better to turn my right flank, though if
we lost we would be cut off from safety. That is a decision that hurts

all through your body; you cannot sleep, you ache. There is nothing more difficult in life."

"Which flank did you turn?"

"My right flank. But that is not important. The decision is important."

"Do you suppose all commanders feel that way? Did Napoleon?"

"Napoleon was a victor. When you are a victor, what can hurt you? But when you must fight a long defensive action with no chance of winning, only of holding the enemy off, then with every decision you are in hell," said Duran. "You ache with wanting—but what you want cannot quite be reached. It is like my sitting in this chair wanting to rip that necktie from your neck. I reach, I almost seize it. It is just beyond my hand. Always in war there are possibilities plain to be seen, but materials are lacking, the men fail, a mistake is made somewhere along the line—and frustration eats your stomach."

It was suggested that perhaps because the military decision is so difficult to make, that is why when it is made rightly it pays off so well. There is nothing in finance, for example, to compare with it, or in internal politics, and perhaps for twenty years the importance of the military decision has been underestimated and aims that are practically inferior have been mistakenly rated above the real pay-off, which still is strength at arms. Hemingway exclaimed: "That's what the new novel is about!" and then another visitor arrived, and the talk took another turn.

Much of the conversation ran to questions of survival or failure to survive. "Where is so-and-so?" "He went back to Russia and was shot." "And so-and-so?" "He also was shot." Another Spanish fighter had landed in a German concentration camp. A married pair "tried to get to Chile but were turned away. They finally were admitted to Buenos Aires." Duran himself escaped from Spain aboard a British destroyer, was taken to Marseille, transported across France in a sealed train, and shipped to England. He was on his way here during the Blitzkrieg in Flanders.

"The world now is very confusing. It is amazing how sure we once were, Ernest, that our ideas were right."

"The fight in Spain will have to be fought again," Hemingway said.

Duran looked at his hands.

"I don't know."

Telephone calls, visitors ushered in and out, another rather hesitant question about writing and another apology to Duran.

"The thing wrong with *To Have and Have Not* is that it is made of short stories. I wrote one, then another when I was in Spain, then I came back and saw Harry Morgan again and that gave me the idea for a third. It came out as a new novel, but it was short stories, and there is a hell of a lot of difference. A novel—when you do a novel"—he couldn't find the phrase he wanted. "I don't know how many more I'll do. But they say that when you're in your forties you ought to know enough and have enough stuff to do one good one. I think this is it."

After his long session of work Hemingway looked elephant-big, enormously healthy. His talk is unevenly paced, a quick spate and then a slow search for a word. His chair keeps hitching across the floor toward the other chairs, and then as he reaches a point, a conclusion, he shoves his chair back to the edge of the group again. While Duran was telephoning in the next room he said that Duran was a character in the new novel, which is set in Spain during the civil war, and that while he was writing the book he badly wanted to see Duran, "to straighten things out, to get information."

"Now that I've finally found him the book is on its way to the printer, can't be changed. But I've questioned him and the stuff I used was all right. You write what should be true as, with what knowledge you have, it seems to you. And that's the best you can do, anyway."

Back to His First Field

Kansas City Times/1940

Reprinted, by permission, from the *Kansas City Times* (26 November 1940), 1–2.

Ernest Hemingway stood in his cowman's boots in a room at the Hotel Muehlebach last night, the rain beating against the east windows, remembering the Kansas City of twenty-odd years ago—how Southwest boulevard slanted and how he lay under a Ford while detectives shot two internal revenue agents and how you could sleep in the old pressroom bathtub if your knees articulated properly and how when the fog came in the fall, you could see Hospital hill pushing up, almost smelling its antiseptic concord of odors.

Most of all, said Hemingway, he remembered the old "Style Book" on *The Star* where he had taken his first reporting job and how its platform was clarity, conciseness and accuracy. Except for the first two weeks of his employment, when he was mistaken by the rest of the staff for the extremely youthful but brilliant new dramatic critic occupying a rear desk, an error even the city editor seemed to share, he was on the run. When business was discussed, it seemed to Hemingway that the topic always hove to clarity, conciseness and accuracy.

"Those were the best rules I ever learned for the business of writing," Hemingway said. "I've never forgotten them. No man with any talent, who feels and writes truly about the thing he is trying to say, can fail to write well if he abides with them.

"When I joined the American ambulance corps, in the first World war, I couldn't see well enough to pass the examination. Halley Dickey was on the staff and he went to headquarters and read the placard until he memorized it. He came back and I learned it from him. Then I went to Italy and drove an ambulance."

Hemingway began talking about the Italian militaristic mind. He remembered that nation's many modern routs—Adowa at the fag-end of the nineteenth century; Caporetto, where he himself was with the Italian army; Guadalajara, where the Spanish loyalists with virtually no modern equipment sent crack Fascist legions heeling back, and now the attack on Greece.

"Individually," Hemingway said, "the Italians are good soldiers. But the Fascist theory of 'We are invincible' ruins them every time. I believe they are the worst officered the world has known in modern times. If you and I were in an army and our objective, say, was Salina, we would take Salina. But the Italians aren't satisfied with the first objective. They must have the objective that makes them invincible. If they set out from here to take Salina, they would naturally feel that Denver was the true objective."

"The Greeks are good fighters. I saw them as a correspondent in the fight with Turkey after the World war. They were winning until Constantine stepped in and supplanted all his staff with old-line officers. Then they lost, but they lost because they were officered by men who did not understand the war nor the way to win the war, which the Greeks had been winning until then. It was sickening. I remember an English reporter and myself crying when we saw the new Constantine officers directing artillery fire into the midst of their own troops—men who had fought bravely and successfully for a year."

And so, said Hemingway, what the Greeks are doing today to the Fascists fits historically. Italy has been fighting since the day it invaded Ethiopia, a nation he thinks never has succumbed. If the retreat in Albania continues, it is his judgment that only revolution can come to Italy itself unless the Nazis pour divisions in from the north.

"There is hardly an Italian home where death has not come from war in the last seven or eight years," Hemingway said. "Italy lost many men in Spain. The Loyalists would have won that war and this war would not have come had there been any decency from democratic countries in acknowledging merely in supplies the fight against fascism or egoism, such as Mussolini's or Hitler's egoism. Right was on the Loyalist side, and I still believe right, with other factors equal, usually wins."

Mrs. Hemingway, a European correspondent for *Collier's* magazine, whom the author married five days ago in Cheyenne, observed that war is what it is, all right, but hunger is almost as bad. She telephoned for a waiter.

"You go ahead," Hemingway said. "A woman should always eat when she is hungry. I'll wait for Luis and his wife."

Luis, it developed a moment later, is Luis Quintanilla, artist in residence at the University of Kansas City. Mr. and Mrs. Quintanilla had been detained by the task of feeding their 10-month-old child: even a general, a category to which the guest once belonged, said Hemingway, must bow to the hunger of his own child.

The meeting was on the physical side. Hemingway plucked up the bubbling Quintanilla and fastened him with a crotch hold. Mrs. Hemingway slapped the back of the pink-cheeked Mrs. Quintanilla. The talk drifted into Spanish for a few moments after the artist had presented the newly married couple two of his American sketches.

"Luis," said Hemingway later, "went up fast in the Spanish Loyalist army. He was one of the leaders who seized the Montana barracks in Madrid when the war began. He became a general. Later, he was in charge of the counterespionage against the fifth column in Madrid. He did very good work. His brother Fepe was a great soldier, too."

Of his new novel, *For Whom the Bell Tolls*, a best seller and generally regarded as one of the best books any American ever has produced, Hemingway had this to say:

"I worked on it two years. God knows I worked hard. I put everything I had seen and known of the Spanish conflict in it as truly and as cleanly as I could. When I finished it, I took it to New York to the publishers. When I went back to Key West I was so full of it, I thought I could go on writing the story interminably. But it finished as a book where I now think it should.

"I never have written in any sense for a market. I've written what I felt I must write. But no man writing honestly can keep good when he just writes to produce words. Right now there are two things I would like to write, one a story of the Gulf stream. That would be factual like *Death in the Afternoon*. And I would like to write a book for my boys (John, 16 years old; Patrick, 12, and Gregory, 9)."

Hemingway said he was pleased that the studio which purchased *For Whom the Bell Tolls* had selected Gary Cooper to play the

leading role of the American who fought for the Loyalists in the
Spanish civil war. He pointed out that Cooper rather fitted the
character of Robert Jordan: the fictional character was a native of
Montana—lean, somewhat laconic. All these attributes fit Cooper.

As for Mrs. Hemingway, she must report for duty in New York
December 7 and take an assignment to Europe. She does not know
where the field will be.

"At any event," she said, "right now I'm the war correspondent in
the family."

Author in the Forenoon
The New Yorker/1940

Reprinted from *The New Yorker,* 16 (28 December 1940), 10.
Reprinted by permission; © 1940, 1968 The New Yorker Magazine, Inc.

Fortuitous circumstances enabled us last week to interview Ernest
Hemingway, the novelist, and Sidney Franklin, the matador, and at
the same time to watch Mr. Hemingway box six one-minute rounds
with George Brown, a former trainer of prizefighters. These things
came about one forenoon at Mr. Brown's gymnasium on West Forty-
seventh Street, Mr. Hemingway having told us on the telephone that
he was leaving town the next day and was pressed for time, and
having amiably invited us to meet him at Brown's. When we got there
he introduced us to Brown, who was in trunks and sweatshirt, and
we sat on a massage table while Hemingway changed from street
clothes into a long woollen union suit and put on trunks and
sweatshirt over it. In the process he found that he weighed two
hundred and nineteen pounds stripped. "Brown, here, used to train
Greb," said Hemingway. Brown looked at the floor. "This is a good
place," Hemingway said cheerfully. "It's a good place to come if
you're planning to cool somebody, and even if you're not planning to
cool somebody, it's a good place for keeping in shape. I come here
every morning when I'm in New York. I always live a hell of a healthy
life for the first three hours of every day."

We asked him how his new book, *For Whom the Bell Tolls,* was
going. "It's selling so fast it's ridiculous," he said. "My wife and I are
going out to the Orient after Christmas and put some of that dough
back on the line." We complimented him on the reviews the book
had received and he said, "It's a better book than I can write,
actually." Turning to Brown, he asked, "You finished it yet, George?"
and Brown said, "Not quite, Ernie." "Have you got to that fight on
the hill, when El Sordo and his men get wiped out?" asked the
novelist. "Yeah, that's swell," said Brown. Hemingway grinned pleasantly. "I just made the whole book up as I went along," he said. "I

used to say to my wife, 'I think that son of a bitch Pablo is going to steal the dynamite exploder,' and she'd say, 'Don't you know?' " He laughed loudly and naturally, and he and Brown stepped under the ropes and into the ring.

Hemingway and Brown boxed actively for a one-minute round and then took a rest. "See, I'm in a good sweat already," said Hemingway. We asked him about the now-famous device in which he indicated Spanish profanity by putting in the word "obscenity" here and there, and he said it had occurred to him one day during the Spanish war when he was showing two American newspaper-women around and they had asked him to tell them what their Spanish chauffeur had said when a tire blew out. "They both kept after me, but I realized you couldn't explain that kind of talk in English," Hemingway said, "even if you could get by with it, because the words wouldn't sound the way they do in Spanish. So I tried saying to the girls, 'He says obscenity the obscenities of the gearshift of the car's father,' and I decided that would be the way to do it in a book."

Hemingway then fought another one-minute round with Brown and in the middle of the third round Mr. Franklin appeared. "Hey!" yelled the bullfighter. Hemingway stopped boxing, and the two hugged each other and beat each other on the back. We were introduced to Franklin, who told us, while Hemingway and Brown boxed three more rounds, that he had recently come back from Mexico, where he has been bullfighting fairly regularly since he left Spain. Hemingway went to get a shower and a rubdown and Brown said, "He's the strongest guy I ever had, except Firpo. His arms are like iron and his right forearm is something terrific. It's from all that big-game fishing." "He keeps himself in trim, as any successful man does," said Franklin. We walked into the massage room to say goodbye to Hemingway. Lying on his stomach, he told us that it is his habit, when working, to read over every morning what he has written up to that point, and sometimes rewrite a good deal of it, before starting a new page. "This obscenity book got so long it was sometimes two o'clock in the morning before I could start a new page," he said. Franklin came in and sat down and we left them together, reminiscing. "That time going to Spain on the Paris," Hemingway was saying. "The time that obscenity from Hollywood crawled out of that obscenity porthole."

He Was a Right Guy and the Woman with Him Was Good Looking
Stanton Delaplane/1941

Reprinted from the *San Francisco Chronicle* (31 January 1941), 13. © *San Francisco Chronicle*, 1941. Reprinted by permission.

Other reporters want to know: "Is Hemingway a right guy?"

Women want to know: "Is his wife good-looking?"

Well, the answer is "yes" to both.

Hemingway *(For Whom the Bell Tolls)* planed into San Francisco last night by United Air Lines from Los Angeles. The cameras will answer the second question. Reporters who interviewed him will vouch for the first.

Ernest Hemingway and his new wife, Martha Gellhorn, are on their way to China. They sail today on the Matsonia for Hawaii. From there they clipper to Hong Kong, to Chungking, and from there they go down the Burma Road to Rangoon.

"I've had the flu," Hemingway said last night. "I can't hear a thing. You know how these planes close your ears."

Author and wife went into the bar at San Francisco airport for a drink and questioning.

"When will the war be over?" he was asked.

"In three months or 20 years," said Hemingway.

"Now don't say that," said Mrs. Hemingway, "that doesn't sound right."

"Well, that's what I think," said Hemingway.

"Say five years," said Mrs. Hemingway.

"All right, make it five years," said Hemingway.

"What I mean," said Ernest Hemingway, "is that all speculation is nonsense anyway. Either the Germans will take over England by direct assault in three months or it's going to be a long war. That 20 years was just a gag."

Someone said that Somerset Maugham, now in San Francisco, had said that Hemingway ought to stick to short stories. Hemingway laughed.

"Did you hear that?" he asked his wife. His wife hadn't.

"I never met him, but I'd like to," Hemingway said. "What do you want me to do? Do we pose for more photographs or what?"

Mrs. Hemingway said she'd like a scotch and soda. Hemingway said he'd like one, too. Mike Ward and his wife, both of San Francisco, came in and sat down.

"Mike's an old friend of mine from Paris," said Hemingway. They discussed various friends they'd seen recently—Benchley, Donald Ogden Stewart.

"The real reason I'm going out to the Orient," said Hemingway, "is because I've seen a war in Europe, and we were both in Spain two years. She covered the war in Finland, you know."

"If anything big happens, it ought to happen in the Pacific. That is if the Axis is really a working agreement. We wanted to go East for a while."

Hemingway said he is covering for *PM,* the new New York daily, and Mrs. Hemingway is writing for *Collier's.* He has been down in Hollywood looking over preparations for a movie based on *For Whom the Bell Tolls.*

He said he'd like to see Gary Cooper play the part of Robert Jordan, the Loyalist dynamiter in the book. Mrs. Hemingway and Mrs. Ward said they'd like another drink. Hemingway cupped a hand over his ear and said the flu and airplane rides had made him practically deaf.

"A scotch and soda," said Mrs. Hemingway loudly.

"Sure," said the author. "You fellows want to know about Spain. Well, I think Germany will encourage Spain to stay out of the war and collect everything she can from England for staying out."

Everybody got up and said, "Thank you, Mr. Hemingway."

"OK," said Hemingway, "sure you got everything you wanted? I'm no expert on wars, but I'll try."

"I'd like to get a little more," said a reporter.

"Come over to the bar," said Hemingway, "what do you want?"

"I don't know," said the reporter, "but I'd like to get enough for a half a column." (Ed. Note: He got three-quarters.)

"Well, I don't either," said Hemingway, "but have a drink.

"If you think of anything call me at my hotel."

A man like that is really all right.

Hemingway, Here for a Visit, Says He'd Think He Was Slipping If He Had Won Pulitzer Prize

St. Louis Star-Times/1941

Reprinted from the St. Louis Star-Times (23 May 1941), 1.

Ernest Hemingway expressed delight in St. Louis today that he had not won the Pulitzer prize for the best American novel of last year. The author of For Whom the Bell Tolls, a novel which was widely praised and which brought $150,000 for movie rights alone, Hemingway told a reporter:

"If I'd won that prize, I'd think I was slipping. I've been writing for twenty years and never have won a prize. I've gotten along all right."

The Pulitzer prize for the most distinguished novel, usually announced in May, was not awarded this year for the first time since 1920. No reason was given.

When a reporter asked Hemingway how he felt about this, he first explained why he was not chagrined, then remarked: "Why didn't they give it to someone else?"

He was in St. Louis for a brief visit with his wife's mother, Mrs. George Gellhorn of 4366 McPherson Avenue. Recently he toured China with his wife, the writer, Martha Gellhorn. She was not with him here because she had gone on to Batavia to obtain material for a magazine article. Hemingway was en route to New York .

With his sleeves rolled up and thick-rimmed glasses low on his nose, Hemingway was interrupted as he sat writing an article for the New York newspaper PM. His shirt was open at the top, exposing the hairy chest once publicized by Max Eastman, and his face and arms bore a vivid sunburn.

"Got that while fishing off Wake Island in the Pacific," Hemingway said, in the short, meaty style of his novels. "Don't ask me what kind of fish. We didn't catch any."

He said he could not reveal what he had found out in the Orient. "My boss in New York would wonder what he was paying me for, if I told you about it," he added. "I can tell you, though, I am still optimistic about China."

Hemingway, who is slow and easy in manner and a trifle thick in the waist for a man so keen about bull-fighting and big game hunting, shambled over to open a portfolio. He had a photograph of 75,000 Chinese working on an airfield in northern China, building it without machinery, mixing concrete by wading in it and tromping the gravel in, like peasants crushing grapes with their bare feet to make wine.

"What a people!" Hemingway exclaimed.

Of his book *For Whom the Bell Tolls,* which emanated from the war in Spain, Hemingway said: "I waited until the war was over before I wrote it. People kept asking me when I was going to work on it. I wanted Spain to seep in.

"Spain was the keystone. What we have today we wouldn't have had if the war in Spain hadn't ended the way it did. Hitler and Mussolini had to win there first."

Of criticisms that the novel did not give a true picture of the Spanish conflict, and that it was vulgar and obscene, Hemingway said: "Writers can't pay any attention to that sort of thing. You've got to do the job the way you see it."

Asked if he had another novel in mind, he said:

"I suppose I'm always working on a book, but I may not know it. It may come out when 'Marty' and I get back to Cuba."

Story of Ernest Hemingway's Far East Trip

Ralph Ingersoll/1941

Reprinted, by permission of Ralph Ingersoll from *PM* (9 June 1941), 6–10.

This interview with Ernest Hemingway was recorded in his hotel apartment a few days after he returned to New York from the Far East in 1941. Mr. Ingersoll, the editor of the now defunct newspaper *PM,* had commissioned Hemingway to go to the Far East to see for himself whether or not war with Japan was inevitable. This interview served as an introduction to Hemingway's series of articles. It was corrected and revised by Hemingway after having been transcribed and hence might be called an authenticated interview.

Ernest Hemingway left for China in January. He had never been in the Orient before. He went to see for himself—how Chiang Kaishek's war against Japan was going; how much truth there was to the reports that the Chinese position was menaced by threat of civil war; what would be the effect of the then imminent Russo-Japanese pact and—most important of all—what was our own position in the Orient. What was our position both as a leading anti-Fascist power and as a nation of 130,000,000 people with vital trade interests in other parts of the world—or were they vital?—and if they were vital, were they menaced?

Hemingway wanted to find out for himself, and for you and for me, what pattern of events might lead us into war with Japan—what alternate sequence of circumstances might possibly keep Japan in her place in the Pacific without us having to fight her.

Most people know Ernest Hemingway as America's No. 1 novelist. His reputation as a novelist is so great in fact that it overshadows two other reputations, either one of which gives him international recognition.

Long before he was a novelist, Ernest Hemingway was a noted war correspondent. He covered the fighting in the Mediterranean in the last war, the whole of the Spanish war—in which the present war was fought in miniature.

Of sufficient stature to be distinct from his reputation as a war correspondent is his reputation as a military expert. He is a student of war in its totality—everything about war, from machine gun emplacements to tactics and maneuvers to civilian morale and industrial organization for war. These things he has studied for 20 years.

So when Ernest Hemingway went to China he went as no casual visitor but as a student and an expert—he went with a reputation which made it possible for him to visit fronts that had not been visited by foreign journalists until now, and to talk with people who are running the war in the Orient on a unique basis.

When Ernest Hemingway went to the Orient, *PM* made this agreement with him: that if action broke out he was to remain there and cover the war by cable, but if no action broke out, he was to make notes as he went but not to write until he finished this study— until all the returns were in and he had time and the perspective to analyze everything he had seen and heard, and render a report of more lasting value than day-to-day correspondence.

This is the report that will be published here beginning tomorrow.

In the meantime, I have talked with Mr. Hemingway about his trip. Here is where he went and what he did and what he saw—the background from which his report is drawn:

Ernest Hemingway went to China with his wife, Martha Gellhorn. Mrs. Hemingway carried credentials as correspondent for *Collier's* where her articles have already begun appearing. The two flew to Hong Kong by Pan American Clipper.

Hemingway stayed a month in Hong Kong, where he could talk not only with the Chinese but with their opposition. The Japanese come in and out of Hong Kong quite freely—in fact, they celebrated the Emperor's birthday in their frock coats and with a formal toast. The British naval and military intelligence is there—and our own naval and military intelligence. The local Communist opposition is there and so are the Chinese pacifists who play Japan's game.

We asked Hemingway what it is like in Hong Kong. He said that danger had hung over the place so long it had become absolutely

commonplace. People had completely adjusted themselves to the
tension. He said that the city was very gay. The stabilizing element in
any British colony are the British womenfolk, who keep life on a
formal basis. But they had been evacuated and in general morale
was high and morals low.

"There are at least 500 Chinese millionaires living in Hong Kong—
too much war in the interior, too much terrorism in Shanghai to suit a
millionaire. The presence of the 500 millionaires has brought about
another concentration—of beautiful girls from all parts of China. The
500 millionaires own them all. The situation among the less beautiful
girls is very bad because it is the British position that prostitution does
not exist there, and therefore its control is no problem. This leaves
about 50,000 prostitutes in Hong Kong. Their swarming over the
streets at night is a war-time characteristic.

How many troops there are in Hong Kong is, of course, a military
secret. Hemingway knows the exact number. That is the type of
censorship *PM* does not try to beat. But Hemingway reports Hong
Kong is "excellently defended.

"In case of attack Hong Kong's problem would be food. There are
1,500,000 people there now and they would have to be fed."

He continued: "Even more serious would be the sewage disposal
problem—for in Hong Kong there are neither flush toilets nor drains.
Sewage is disposed of by night soil coolies who collect and sell it to
farmers. In case of a blackout sewage will be dumped in the streets
and a cholera epidemic would be inevitable. This is known because
two nights of practice blackout did produce a cholera epidemic.

"At present, however," Hemingway continued, "the food is plentiful and good, and there are some of the finest restaurants in the
world in Hong Kong—both European and Chinese. There's also
horse racing, cricket, rugby, association football."

After Hemingway had been in Hong Kong a month, he and Mrs.
Hemingway flew to NamYung by Chinese air line. This flight took
him over the Japanese lines. From NamYung, the Hemingway drove
to Shaikwan, headquarters of the 7th War Zone.

The Chinese front is divided into eight war zones. Hemingway
chose the 7th because he "wanted to make an intensive study of
what a typical Chinese war zone was like, and the 7th has, ultimately,
the greatest offensive potentiality."

Here he studied the complete organization of a Chinese war zone from headquarters through the army corps, divisions, brigades, regiments and down to the forward echelons.

The army Hemingway visited is a Kuomintang army. That is, it is part of the regular Chinese Army and not part of the Chinese Communist Army. The Chinese Communist armies have welcomed journalists and there has been much written about them. But this is the first time an American journalist has done extensive work at the front with the regular Chinese Army.

We asked Hemingway about this situation. He said:

"There are 300 divisions in the Chinese Army, 200 of which are first-class divisions and 100 secondary divisions. There are 10,000 regular troops in each division. Out of these 300 divisions three are Communist divisions. The area that the Communist divisions hold is an extremely important one and they have done marvelous fighting. But the 297 other divisions, occupying about the same amount of terrain per division, have not been visited at all before. Whereas the Communists have welcomed correspondents, there has been very strict censorship on the regular Chinese Army. Passes have been impossible to get, and correspondents have not been allowed into the forward echelons at all."

Hemingway said he went to see the regular Chinese Army because the Communist troops have already been excellently described by people like Edgar Snow, Agnes Smedley and others.

News of the Kuomintang army is important not simply because it has received no publicity but because the Kuomintang comprises the bulk of the troops on which we, in America, must depend to keep the Japanese divisions occupied in China while we are preparing to defend the Pacific.

Hemingway spent a month at the front, living with the troops, going everywhere with them. He traveled down the river by sampan first, then on horseback, and finally on foot. There were 12 days during a wet spell when he and Mrs. Hemingway never had dry clothes to put on.

They also discovered such delicacies as snake wine and bird wine. Hemingway described snake wine as "a special rice wine with a number of small snakes coiled up at the bottom of the bottle. The snakes are dead," he said. "They are there for medicinal purposes.

Bird wine is also rice wine, but at the bottom of its bottle there are several dead cuckoos."

Hemingway liked the snake wine better. He says it cures falling hair and he is going to have some bottled for his friends.

After a month at the front, the Hemingways went back overland by sampan, car and train to Kweilin. This trip had not been planned, but everywhere they had gone for two months they had been told Kweilin was the most beautiful place in China. And they reported that it is the most beautiful place they saw. "There are thousands of miniature mountains there which look like a huge mountain range but are only 300 feet high. Many of the lovely imaginative scenes you see in Chinese prints and paintings, and think are made up out of an artist's imagination, are really almost photographic likenesses of Kweilin. There is also a famous cave there which is now used for an aid raid shelter. It holds 30,000 people."

To get from there to Chungking they arranged to be picked up by a freight plane which was carrying bank notes to the capital. The plane was a Douglas DC-3—the kind that flies on most of our air lines here—and all the other seats were occupied by shipments of bank notes.

All the air lines in China are owned by a company called the CNAC, or China National Aviation Corp. The Chinese Government owns 51 per cent and our own Pan American Airways owns 49 percent and does the operating. Hemingway said:

"They used DC-2's and 3's and old Condor biplanes which can only fly on short hauls where the mountains are under 7000 feet high. There are passenger flights from Hong Kong to Chungking three times a week, for instance. But the idea of buying tickets on them is an academic one—for the waiting list is months long and only priority counts."

When it did not look as if the priority was coming through in time, Hemingway chartered a Vultee single-motored low-wing monoplane. But then the priority came through.

By the time the Hemingways got to Chungking they had learned a good deal about China. They spent some time with Chiang Kai-shek and in an all-afternoon interview, Mme. Chiang Kai-shek did the interpreting. But Hemingway reports that when the talk was on military subjects the Generalissimo understood military terms in

English. He saw and got to know China's Minister of Finance, Dr. Kung, the Minister of Education, the Minister of Communications, the Minister of War, as well as various generals and the General Staff.

"Chungking," he reports, "had not been bombed seriously from August 25 until May 3—there is no bombing in Chungking during the winter because of low visibility."

He found the hotels in Chungking excellent—the food plentiful and the water hot. Everywhere he went in China, in fact, he found food sold without restrictions—even in the villages. At no time, he reports, did he see any of the signs you see when the war is being lost for lack of food. At no time did he see anything like the conditions he saw in Spain.

"But," he said, "the food in China is expensive. Moreover, China is such a huge country that there are sections where the food situation gets bad locally—when due to a local drought a crop has failed. And communications are so bad that it is difficult to ship in food from other parts of the country. Such a condition prevails at present in South Shansi province and in other parts of the northern provinces. On the whole, the food situation this year is very good.

We asked Hemingway what people meant when they came back and said the economic situation in China was "very bad."

He said: "When people come into China from America and see signs of a monetary inflation there, they think everything is going to pot, whereas the situation is actually very good, considering China is in the fourth year of war. The inflation there is no worse than occurs in any other country that fights for fours years. In the fourth year of the last war no European country was in better shape."

He felt that "China has to make some radical currency reforms—but principally to prevent the Japanese from buying up their money. The Japanese sell their own money short and buy Chinese money—now that America is backing China's money," he said. "I don't think this will be hard to control. My personal opinion is that eventually China will have to adjust its currency on a rice standard. Rice is the gold of China and only a currency based on a rice standard will prevent the kind of inflation in which people are not able to buy food."

The first time the Hemingways were in Chungking they stayed

about eight days, constantly talking with people. Hemingway dined, lunched and breakfasted with Government people.

At the end of the eight days he flew up to Chengtu to visit the Chinese military academy—where Chiang Kai-shek trains his officers and cadets. And he inspected the flying schools and the new airdromes that are being constructed in this district. Here again, as a guest of the military academy, he had an opportunity to study the whole Chinese military system.

"The military academy," he said, "is in full swing. It was set up by a German General Alexander Von Faulkenhausen, and its professors are German-trained Chinese."

Hemingway flew back from the Chinese West Point to Chungking and then took another plane south over the Burma Road. He saw the trucks passing up and down the road.

We asked him whether reports that the Road was all banged up were true. He said: "Some of the bridges were out, but the Chinese have a very efficient ferry system to replace them. The Road is being bombed regularly—Kunming practically every day—but the bombing of bridges is not effective, partly because of the ferries and partly because they rebuild the bridges so quickly."

Hemingway said: "The control organization of the China section of the Burma Road is now in the charge of a committee which includes Dr. Harry Baker, former head of the American Red Cross in China. If Dr. Baker is not hamstrung by his fellow committee members he will be able to put through many traffic reforms."

From Lashio, which, you will see by the map, is far up on the Burma Road route, Hemingway went to Mandalay by car and then down to Rangoon by train. All along this route he studied the Burma Road problem, and gave us this picture of it:

"The first part of the problem is getting materials from the coast up to the beginning of the Road. Here there are two methods of transportation available. One is via the Burma railway, the other is via the river. So far most of the material has gone up over the railway which is Burmese owned and very jealous of river traffic. The river traffic is transported by an organization called the Irrawaddy Flotilla, which belongs to a Scottish-owned company.

"The Irrawaddy is navigable as far as Bhamo. You should look at

the map here because Bhamo is becoming very important. At Bhamo
a connecting road is being completed through to the Burma Road.
You will see that not only does it cut off a good part of the Burma
Road—and a difficult and mountainous part—but it permits goods to
be transported up from the coast all the way by river. In effect this
new route—from Rangoon to Bhamo by water and from Bhamo by
short cut to well up on the Burma Road—constitutes a cut-off which
is almost impossible for the Japanese to damage.

"The old route," he continued, "by rail from Lashio to Kunming,
remains available, and shippers can also use the river up from
Rangoon to Mandalay to Lashio.

"This makes two ways in.

"A third way," he went on, "is now being developed. This way uses
first water and then rail to a place called Myitkyina—pronounced
Michina—which, if you are interested in the Burma Road problem,
you should locate for yourself on the map. Because you will see that
by using Myitkyina as a railhead, a 200-mile air shuttle service from
Myitkyina to Tali cuts off 509 miles of the Burma Road and leaves
only 197 miles to travel to Kunming.

"This 197 miles—from Tali to Kunming—is downhill and there are
no bridges and gorges which the Japanese can turn into bottlenecks
by bombing. On a 200-mile hop the freight planes will not have to
refuel in China at all.

"Thus," Hemingway explained, "the Chinese have what amounts
to three alternate routes of supply from the south, not counting the
constant bootlegging of supplies in from the whole China Coast."

Hemingway studied this traffic and says it is of enormous extent.
He does not write about it in detail because he does not want to give
information to the Japanese.

Now, remembering that the overland route into Russia is still open
and that the Chinese are still getting supplies from Russia—as
Hemingway explains in one of his articles—one realizes for the first
time just what an enormous problem the Japanese have in interrupting Chinese communications.

"If the Japanese interruptions on the Road were as one, the
interruptions due to inefficiency, graft and red tape would be as five.
That is, take the whole route from Rangoon into Chungking—

inefficiency, graft and red tape cause five times as much trouble as Japanese bombings. This is the problem which Dr. Baker has to solve."

We were startled by this figure and asked Hemingway to tell us more about it. He said:

"All projects in China move very quickly until money is involved. The Chinese have been doing business for many centuries and when things are a business matter to them they move very slowly. The Generalissimo can order something done—something in which money doesn't enter—and it is done practically, immediately. But the minute it becomes a financial thing it slows right up. No one person is responsible for this. It is the age-old Chinese custom of squeeze.

"There have been cases of truck drivers selling their gasoline, which they were hauling over the Burma Road, to private concerns. There have been cases of dumping whole loads to carry passengers. I saw with my own eyes tires being thrown off trucks loaded with them—evidently to be picked up by confederates later.

"There's no efficient policing of the Road. Of course every load should be checked as it goes in, and all the way through, and as it comes out. That is what Dr. Baker's Commission has to fix. After they opened the Road things ran wild for a while. Some people, operating transportation companies from outside of China, had no efficient control of their organizations on the Road. Now the Generalissimo realizes the importance of this. Something is being done about it."

Hemingway told us that the situation in Burma doesn't make things any better. He said: "Burma is a land of complete and utter red tape. Everything there is slowed up as much as it can be. If a military attaché comes to Rangoon to get a load of food to take back up to Kunming, it takes him two days in Rangoon just to clear through red tape. It is worse than France was before the fall. It is entirely administered by the Burmese, who combine the worst features of the Hindu Babu and the French pre-fall functionary. On the other hand, the British in Burma, not the Burmese, were efficient and uniformly helpful. Censorship was realistic and intelligent."

We asked Hemingway what it was like visiting romantic-sounding places like Mandalay and Rangoon. He said Rangoon was an English colonial city, "96 degrees at night and 103 degrees in the day, in the hot months when we were there. The flying fish were not playing. Kipling was talking about a place further down—Moulmein, below Rangoon, near the mouth of the river."

Hemingway went all the way down to Rangoon and stayed there for about a week. Then he flew back via Lashio and Kunming to Hong Kong and stayed there again for a week before leaving for America. Mrs. Hemingway continued on to Batavia and the Dutch East Indies while Hemingway worked between Clippers in Manilla. She rejoined him on the next Clipper.

As this is being written Mr. Hemingway is completing his last piece for *PM*. We asked him a few final questions: What about the Chinese arsenals? If, by any mischance, the supply routes were cut, could they go on fighting?

He said: "I visited arsenals near Chungking and saw that they were manufacturing small arms and small arms ammunition, and were very self-sufficient. Moreover, much material can come right through Japanese lines. The guerrillas had been running trucks through the Japanese lines by completely dismantling them—into the smallest possible pieces—and carrying them by hand. An American motor company representative in Hong Kong was delivering trucks through the Japanese lines to Free China making a $450 service charge for delivery." Hemingway has more news of the latest developments in guerrilla fighting.

News from the Orient has been confusing and contradictory to most people. Russia supposedly offers the hand of friendship to Japan—and at the same time continues to ship supplies to China.

America gives China a $100,000,000 credit—and at the same time sells oil to China's enemy. What's it all about?

Hemingway told us. He traced for us the probable consequences of each move we were making, and each Japanese move.

He showed us how Russia was playing a devious hand in this gigantic game of Chinese checkers which anybody might win.

Must America fight Japan? Hemingway told us why it's a matter of timing. As far as America is concerned, time itself is fighting on our side. As for Japan, time is running out on her—and no one, not even the Japanese, knows when the last strategic moment will have come. Or whether she should extricate herself from China at any price before challenging us. If Britain should fall it would be the signal for

Japan aggressively to pursue her conquests in new directions. And this may well mean war with the U.S.A.

If England grows stronger and America is able to keep the fleet in the Pacific, war between the United States and Japan may never occur. And further, Hemingway tells us, we may thus beat Japan without ever firing a gun.

No one interview such as this, however—no one article—can give you the full impact, can piece together the complete pattern of this tremendously significant picture.

They Call Him Papa

Mary Harrington/1946

Reprinted, by permission, from the *New York Post Week-End Magazine* (28 December 1946), 3.

They call Ernest Hemingway Papa. Maybe that's because he's father of our modern American literary style. But more likely it's because he's a little bigger, more alive and warmer than anyone else in any room he enters.

And his wife, Mary Welsh, a war correspondent, looks so much like Maria of *For Whom the Bell Tolls* that you expect her to speak Spanish.

They're a good combination. Hemingway is a tremendous man, and she's tiny and lithe. Both have seen war and both want a little quiet. And she wants to make him happy. They met in Paris during the war and were married last March 15.

The Hemingways are at their home now, 12 miles from Havana. But before they left, they spent four hours with this reporter in their Sherry-Netherland Hotel suite.

Papa wore gray flannel slacks and a blue oxford cloth shirt. His tan leather moccasins were a little run down. Because there was company, he put on a long plaid tie. At 47, Hemingway looks virile enough to make bobby soxers swoon by the droves.

A massive man, he wears iron-rimmed spectacles issued by the Army when he was in China in 1941. His dark hair is graying at the temples, and there is gray in the bushy mustache, too. His voice is low, and he talks quickly.

His gestures are those of a boxer and his movements as graceful as a bullfighter's. Mary, whom he calls Kitner, is blonde, blue-eyed, wears sweaters and skirts most of the time. And what she obviously likes best to do is to get her husband talking and then just listen.

Back in Havana, he will finish a book, 1,200 pages of which he has written. He won't tell what it is about, and no one has seen it, but it is rumored that the movies have bought it—unseen—for $250,000. It's probably about World War II.

"It's a big book," Hemingway says. "I've broken the back of it now. I'd like to write a good novel and 10 or 15 more short stories and not go to any more wars. I'd like to raise my kids."

While he finishes the book, Mary will keep house, redecorate, fix up a garden. She isn't writing anything for a year, she says, because she's tired. He gets up at seven every morning and writes till lunch time. She sleeps late and then swims a half mile in their pool. The rest of the day is theirs.

It is, of necessity, a quiet time for them. Mary has been ill and is taking it easy, and Hemingway conditions himself for writing as one of his fictional bull fighters before a big day.

"Writing a novel is like a six-day bicycle race," he says. "A novel is a long thing. Like the bike race, only it goes on for two years."

That's why he moved to Cuba. In Key West, there were too many people he knew too well. And Papa is no man to shirk a party or leave friends at a bar. He likes people too well.

"A writer can't say he's busy," he says. "No conferences to go to. So now we live just far enough from town so when the guys get drunk and decide to go see Ernest, it's too long a trip. And we got no phone."

How does he work? At a tiny desk in a far wing of the house. In a room where there's a massive, Hemingway-type desk. He writes in longhand with a stubby pencil. And every page is a tremendous effort. For writing doesn't come easy with Hemingway.

"He has this great big gorgeous desk," Mary says. "And he doesn't use it."

"What do I need a big desk for?" her husband asks. "For more confusion? To spread more bills on it?"

And he's not worried about his new book. He's like a tightrope walker who can't afford to look down.

"I've thrown away plenty of stuff in my time," he says. "When you spend all your life learning how to write, you can't let yourself think it'll be bad. And if anybody tells me they didn't like one of my books, I just give them their money back."

He's almost afraid of flattery and seems shy about it. Please don't say that unless you mean it, he tells the person who would compliment him. And he disagrees with the critics who call him the greatest living American writer. History probably will prove him wrong, but he'll take Faulkner any day, he says.

"William Faulkner is the best living," he says. "And Nelson Algren *(Never Come Morning)*. His other literary favorites are Flaubert, Bordeler*, Mark Twain, Henry James and Stephen Crane.

Hemingway is a master hunter, has even hunted lions in Africa. It's his hobby and he recently returned from shooting at Sun Valley. His youngest son, Gregory, has won prizes in marksmanship. Papa is very proud of that.

Every Hemingway admirer knows he's a man who has as much of what he calls guts as do any of his heroes. Born in 1899, he ran away from his Oak Park, Ill., home to become a prize-fighter. His doctor-father persuaded him to come back, and he finished high school. Instead of college, he went to work for the *Kansas City Star*. But the year was 1917 and it was war, so at 19, Hemingway joined an ambulance unit bound for Italy.

He transferred to the infantry. A mortar shell hit him, and he still wears a silver kneecap. In 1921 he came back to America and married Hadley Richardson, his boyhood sweetheart. They went to Paris. Those were the lean years for him.

No one wanted to buy his short stories. They had a son, John, now 22, who was a paratroop captain and was captured by the Germans during the last war. He is now at the University of Montana.

Several years later, in Spain, the country he knows better than his own, Hemingway became a Catholic to marry Pauline Pfeiffer, but they split over the Spanish War when she favored the Catholic Franco. They had two sons, Patrick, now 17, and Gregory (Mousey), now 15—the business head in the family. Hemingway's third wife, the writer Martha Gellhorn, who covered the Spanish War with him, divorced him last December.

Mary, born in Bimidji, Minnesota, attended Northwestern University and then went to work for the *Chicago Daily News*. Lord Beaverbrook hired her for his *London Daily Express* and she went there in 1937, later marrying Noel Monks, a London newspaperman.

*Presumably the newspaper's rendering of "Baudelaire"—MJB.

They were divorced last year. She covered the war for *Time* magazine.

Pretty Mary laughs when asked what it's like to be Mrs. Hemingway.

"It's entertaining," she says. "I always want to have as much fun as I'm having now. Being married is much nicer than being single. You can have an awful lot of fun if you're single, and you don't have to pick up somebody else's socks. But it's not the same."

Mary's having cook trouble though. The cook speaks only Chinese, and "no other known language."

"I'm buying lots of seeds for the garden, and I'm redecorating like mad," she says. "It's a good life. It's THE good life."

Hemingway is more matter-of-fact.

"What's a good place to live?" he asks. "Any place you work and make a good living is a good place. I don't need much, not as much as I have, just enough to get by while I'm writing."

And he's inclined—with obvious sincerity—to minimize his success. His explanation of why people read him is:

"Because I sound like the 'L' and they've taken the 'L' away."

Both Hemingways, Kitner and Papa himself, think this is their last marriage. They deserve happiness, too.

And for the thousands of readers who wondered about the sleeping bag in *For Whom the Bell Tolls,* Hemingway has it.

"It's double," he says. "You can spread it out for two, if you want."

On the Books

Roger Bourne Linscott/1946

Reprinted from the *New York Herald Tribune Book Review* (29 December 1946), 13. © I.H.T. Corporation. Reprinted by permission.

Ernest Hemingway, who is nearing fifty but still looks and talks like the vigorous heroes whom you've met in some of his books, returned to New York two weeks ago after a bout of duck-shooting on Long Island and almost immediately took off for a Christmas in Cuba, his home since 1938.

The duck-shooting, he told me when I talked to him shortly before his final departure, was "pretty lousy," but on the subject of his new novel, which he has been working on since the start of the year, he was somewhat more cheerful. "It's a little more than half written," he reported. "I've done about 1,200 manuscript pages and I expect to give it at least nine months' more work before I'm through with it. I'm taking my time and writing as good a book as I can." As to subject matter, he described it as "another long novel, touching on the war," although it is not written (like *A Farewell to Arms*) in the first person.

Not as fast a writer as you might think from his easy style, Mr. Hemingway works on a strict schedule that produces an average of 500 to 1,000 words a day. "I start in at seven in the morning," he says, "and I always quit when I'm going good, so that I'll be able to pick right up again the next day." He migrated to Cuba from Key West, his home in the middle thirties, when a W.P.A.-built highway made the Keys too accessible to visitors. "I have to have enforced discipline," he explains, "or I just don't get any writing done. The trouble is I like to see people, and a writer doesn't have an office organization to protect him from friends the way a business man does."

Looking backward from the vantage point of 1946, Hemingway considers "The Snows of Kilimanjaro," which he wrote nearly ten years ago, "about as good as any of my stories." "I haven't read any of my novels in a long time," he says, "but I suppose that I got the biggest kick out of writing *The Sun Also Rises*. It was my first real novel, and I didn't know whether I could do it or not."

As a leading spokesman for the "lost generation" of writers who emerged from the first world war, Mr. Hemingway, unlike a good many other observers, doesn't feel that World War II will produce the quality of disillusioned realism that characterized American writing in the '20s. "Some very excellent writing is going to come out of this war by writers who are completely unknown right now," he says, "but it's going to be entirely different from what we had before. There were plenty of things the matter with this war, but it was still a lot better run than the first one. Things happened quickly—there weren't any of those blunders and long delays that made you feel that it was all just a gigantic conspiracy. I'm not very well up on recent American writing, but I've seen some post-war French stuff that's excellent. Especially some stories by Jean-Paul Sartre—a collection called *Le Mur*. It's first-rate writing."

Expatriatism, he feels, is pretty much of a closed chapter in American writing, at least until the cost of living in Europe takes a drop. "The reason writers went to France in the '20s," he says, "was because we could live so much more cheaply there, not because we had any particular desire to leave this country. It's just a matter of economics."

Indestructible

The New Yorker/1947

Reprinted from *The New Yorker*, 22 (4 January 1947), 20.
Reprinted by permission; © 1947, 1975 The New Yorker Magazine, Inc.

Ernest Hemingway has been spending a few weeks in and around town—overcompensating for an infantile aversion to death by duck shooting on Long Island Sound, boxing at Stillman's Gym, and otherwise playing the part of the fictional character of the same name who appears regularly in the prose works of Earl Wilson and Leonard Lyons—and toward the end of his visit we arranged to meet him at a midtown restaurant for lunch. Though we have been trained to regard all literary figures as an infirm and pitiable lot, we must confess that when Mr. Hemingway bounded through the restaurant doorway, we got the impression that he had just happily carved his way in through a mob of bloody and fanatical Igorots. We were gratified to note that despite the weather, which was cold and blustery, he was wearing only an old tweed jacket and gray flannel trousers. "Don't own an overcoat," he told us, squeezing our hand hard in an indication of heaven knows what basic sense of insecurity. "Don't need one. Not a bad day out."

Mr. Hemingway struck us as being of slightly larger than human proportions, and his resemblance to a handsome, playful, and potentially violent bear was heightened by the way his hair ran down over his coat collar like a shaggy gray pelt. On his forehead is a coin-shaped scar, which he got in an automobile accident in London during the war, but except for this he looks and acts indestructible—a state of affairs that neatly supports his theory that no Hemingway ever dies a natural death. "That's one reason I've written so little about my family," he told us over a couple of Martinis and a dish of snails. "I can't say everything I want to say about my family as long as certain people are still alive. Maybe I'll never get to write much about it, but maybe by the time I'm through, I'll have done enough

48

work, so it won't matter." He was, he announced, approximately halfway through a new novel. "I've finished eighty-seven thousand words," he said, "but I haven't cut it yet and I always cut a lot. I don't want to say what the book is about, because a book you talk about is a book you don't write." We asked him if he found that writing got any easier as time went on. "Not easier," he said, "but it's what I like to do better than anything in the world, and what I have to do. I rewrite so much that the first chapter of a book may be rewritten forty or fifty times; that's just hard work. It's this way, see—when a writer first starts out, he gets a big kick from the stuff he does, and the reader doesn't get any; then, after a while, the writer gets a little kick and the reader gets a little kick; and, finally, if the writer's any good, he doesn't get any kick at all and the reader gets everything."

The only publication that would print his early stories, Mr. Hemingway said, was the *Frankfurter Zeitung,** with the result that they were published in German several years before they appeared in English. "I wrote my first novel, *The Sun Also Rises,* in six weeks, when I was twenty-seven," he continued. "I wrote it because all my friends had written novels and I was ashamed of not having written one. It was written in the first person, which is a cinch; anybody can write a novel in the first person. I didn't make much of anything out of my stuff until quite late. Now I'm sort of a property, the only property my family has, and they're anxious for this new book to be a big success."

Mr. Hemingway finished off the last of a dozen snails and got to his feet. "Have to cut over to the Alvin and see Bergman," he told us as we hurried after him. "She's an old friend of mine. She was in the movie of *For Whom the Bell Tolls,* but I'd better not tell you what I thought of that." When we stepped into the street, he turned up his coat collar and tucked his hands in his pockets. "I hate plays," he said. "Did you ever listen to the dialogue of a play with your eyes shut?" Then he lowered his head into the wind and said, "It's cold. It's colder than I thought————this cold!"

*Hemingway's work appeared in the *Frankfurter Zeitung* in 1927, but *Der Querschnitt* had published his work earlier in Germany—MJB.

Hemingway in the Afternoon

Ernest Hemingway/1947

Reprinted from *Time*, 50 (4 August 1947), 80.

Most of the authors who answered TIME's questions on the state of U.S. writing were interviewed by correspondents. Ernest Hemingway answered his questions by mail. He requested that both TIME's questions & his answers be published "since this has to do with my trade. You can say that when you saw me I was unshaven, needed a haircut, was barefoot, wearing a pyjama bottom and no top." The questions, and his replies:

Q: What do you find wrong with present-day writing—or good about it? Why aren't we getting more significant writing?
A: "Really good writing very scarce always. When comes in quantities everybody very very lucky."
Q: Has postwar or atomic era had any influence on writers; has it had a tendency to dry them up creatively?
A: "Writers dry up when their juice dries up. Atomic bomb probably as fatal to writers as cerebral hemorrhage or senility. Meantime good writers should keep on writing."
Q: Which U.S. writers in your opinion are doing good work?
A: "Writers my generation mostly dead except Dos Passos, going very good with *Number One*. Robert Penn Warren writing very well. First rate books by new writers that have read are *All Thy Conquests*, Alfred Hayes—*Never Come Morning*, Nelson Algren—*The Big Sky*, A. B. Guthrie Jr.—*The Assault*, Allen R. Matthews."
Q: Which once-prominent ones have slipped or failed to measure up to early promise?
A: "Prefer not to answer this question. A writer has no more right to inform the public of the weaknesses and strengths of his fellow professionals than a doctor or a lawyer has.

"Writers should stick together like wolves or gypsies and they are fools to attack each other to please the people who would exploit or destroy them. Naturally I know the weaknesses of my fellow professionals but that information is not for sale nor for free."

Q: How much has the big money of slicks, Hollywood, radio, etc., taken writers away from serious personal themes?

A: "Most whores usually find their vocations."

Q: Is a writer-Hollywood combination capable of doing good literary work?

A: "So far hasn't. But Hollywood has proven can make good pictures from good stories honestly written."

Q: What is your own attitude toward writing for Hollywood?

A: "Never done it."

Q: Do you detect any trends, or any new schools in recent U.S. writing? If so, what are they?

A: "Ask a professor."

Q: Has the "Hemingway influence" declined? If so, what kind of writing are we heading for?

A: "Hemingway influence only a certain clarification of the language which is now in the public domain."

Notes From a Novelist
on His System of Work

Ernest Hemingway/1949

I believe Mr. Cortesi* explained to you why I was unable to answer your letter sooner.

Now, reading it over, I see it would take several thousand words of carefully considered writing to attempt an answer to all the things you bring up.

Let's give my personal life a miss. The only important things are that I should keep healthy and write as well as I can. This is my program for 1949 and as long after as possible.

A long time ago I found it was bad to discuss work you are engaged on. I know it does not work that way with all writers. But that is the way it works with me. It is not followed to be rude nor to be mysterious. It is a system of working.

Discussing other writers for publication is distasteful. Any good professional writer knows the strong points and the weaknesses of the other professionals. He is not under any obligation to point them out to the other writer's reading public. If the other writer is read the public must find the good in him. I see no reason to try to put him out of business by disillusioning anyone he may mystify.

Then, too, if a writer became a critic or entered other fields it could lead to grave humiliations. Imagine not being able to get your fast ball by Truman Capote or dropping a close decision to some Brooklyn Tolstoy. Think of how it could shake a writer's confidence to lose the Secretariat of Agriculture to Louis Bromfield in some little smoke-filled room or wake some morning to find that it was André Malraux who was managing De Gaulle instead of you or that Jean-Paul Sartre

*The *New York Times* forwarded a questionnaire to Hemingway through Rome correspondent Arnoldo Cortesi—MJB.

had won the hand of Simone De Beauvoir while you had been left at the post in the Fifth at Aqueduct. No, I think it is better just to write.

I once read an excellent book by Maxwell Geismar on American writing in which he knew so much about how and why I wrote that he had me groggy for what seemed like a decade (the smallest term used in Big Time Literature). How does Hemingway do it? I would mutter This way? Or like Geismar says?

Finally I decided just to keep my left hand out and keep moving around and wait for Geismar to throw again. Maybe he can hit me with that same punch. Maybe he's got something new now. I want to make him throw though. Because if I keep on writing I can always hit him with a book.

I'm sorry I can't write that sort of piece with the writer's Views on things, and the Literary Scene, and which are my favorite books (the answer to that is the ones with the stiff covers) etc. because this ship is half way between Funchal, Madeira, and La Guayra, Venezuela, and there is a big wallowing, following sea and am writing this in the Chief Engineer's cabin and anyway I doubt if I could write it if I had an office of my own in the Chrysler Building and paid somebody to write it for me.

You're welcome to this though if it is any good to you and if you print any paragraphs from it please print them entire and as they are.

Yours very truly,

ERNEST HEMINGWAY.

Hemingway Novel of Venice Completed at Home in Cuba

Ben F. Meyer/1950

Reprinted, by permission of the Associated Press, from the *Kansas City Star* (10 September 1950), 1.

When I die," says Ernest Hemingway, "it will be from writing checks."

"Not," he added, "that any one will string me up for writing hot ones, but from some sort of ailment growing out of overexercise of the wrist. It seems that I write checks most of the time."

Actually the novelist must have overemphasized a bit the labor of paying bills for he has been very busy for almost two years on his new novel, *Across the River and Into the Trees,* which was published this week. Its setting is Venice.

And how does he think the new book compares with *For Whom the Bell Tolls,* the story of the Spanish war that brought him his greatest fame and wealth?

"I'm crazy about the new book," he said. "I'd go hang myself if I thought it wasn't better. I read the book 206 times, to try and better it or correct errors, and it is as good as I can make it.

"It's different, of course. You can't go writing another book about a bunch of people on a hill in a war. I'd say the new book is about love and death, happiness and sorrow and the town of Venice."

He grinned and added: "I really fired all the barrels on this one."

And what's he doing now that the new novel, first since *For Whom the Bell Tolls,* is out of the way?

"Oh, I'm on another one already. As a matter of fact, I started it a long time ago, and put it aside for this new one. No, I can't work on two at the same time. The one I'm doing now is a very long book. In fact, it's so long the doctors wonder if it may not be too long for me."

His appearance, however, does not suggest that his 51 years are weighing on him. At first glance, he does seem older, but that's because of his moustache, and a full graying beard.

He leads an active life at times working on his farm. His writing day runs from dawn until past noon. After lunch there is usually a fishing trip on his yacht, Pilar, and if luck is good, he spends the afternoon and part of the night fighting marlin. Other days he goes hunting, or to a near-by trap shoot range, or does odd jobs around his place.

The novelist stands just over six feet and, as he says, "I grew out a little on the sides." He is a big barrel-chested man.

He spent twenty-one months on *Across the River and Into the Trees.*

"I have thin eyelids, and the first light of dawn wakes me up, so I go to work, and stay at it until a little after noon. After lunch, I usually go fishing. Presently I've got to go to the dentist for a check-over."

He put the scene of the new book in Venice because "I sort of grew up around there as a kid. I couldn't go there while Mussolini was around, but I went back soon after he wasn't. I like the place."

A cat strolled up, stretched, and sat down on Hemingway's left foot. There seemed to be a number of them around.

"There are fifty-two cats, and two dogs," he said. "That's the latest house count."

The gate to Hemingway's house is two blocks off the central highway, which runs from one end of Cuba to the other. His place is just at the edge of this village, which is about ten miles from downtown Havana. He spends little time there, except to go for his yacht, which is anchored in Havana harbor. He shuns the social life in Cuba's gay capital.

Some time ago he attended an outdoor luncheon honoring the duke and duchess of Windsor. He horrified some of the women by going in shorts, which are his standard dress. But the duke and duchess did not seem disturbed and Hemingway sat for an hour or so chatting with the duchess.

Once in a while he eats lunch at the International Nautical club, where he keeps his boat. Visitors from all over the world come to the Hemingway house. Friends are always welcome, but not the curious. there is a sign on the gate in Spanish saying that only those with appointments will be received.

Trees and tropical shrubs and flowers almost hide the house from the street. He lives there with his wife, the former Mary Welsh of Bemidgi, Minn. Both enjoy fishing. Mrs. Hemingway recently won first prize in the Havana International Marlin Fishing tournament, with a 100-pounder.

Besides fishing, Hemingway enjoys poker, hunting, trap shooting, popular music. He has his pet hates, too. One of them is canasta. "I never play it. Hell, I'm a card player."

He writes where the notion strikes him. Some of it is done in longhand—"the scenery, and the descriptive stuff. For conversation, I use the typewriter, so it doesn't get too far ahead of me."

He speaks little of his books. He picked up the jacket on his new book, looked at the picture of himself on the back cover. "It's a good picture, even if it makes me look like the devil. It's the only picture, though, that shows very distinctly the three places where my nose was broken."

That seemed to please him.

"Hemingway Is Bitter about Nobody"
—but His Colonel Is

Ernest Hemingway/1950

Reprinted from *Time,* 56 (11 September 1950), 110.
Copyright 1950 Time Inc. All rights reserved. Reprinted by
permission from *Time.*

Last year, in a rare revelation of his writing plans,
Ernest Hemingway let it be known that he was
writing a short novel, *Across the River and into the
Trees.* He was sidetracking work on a much longer
novel to do so; the idea had come to him while
recovering from serious illness. U.S. book circles
were fascinated. As the story had it, Hemingway
wanted to get some things down on paper that he
had never managed to say before; *Across the River*
was going to be the Hemingway credo in a nutshell.
When a magazine version of the book appeared in
Cosmopolitan earlier this year, it raised other questions. Wasn't the novel's hero a pretty thinly dis-
guised version of Hemingway himself? What was
Hemingway trying to say about Allied commanders
in World War II? And—in view of the book's flaws—
was Hemingway satisfied with it?
TIME cabled some of these questions to Novelist
Hemingway. His reply, cabled from Cuba:

Hemingway was ill with erysipelas, streptococcus, staphylococcus
and anthrax infections in Cortina d'Ampezzo and in hospital in
Padova, English spelling Padua. Received 13 million units of penicillin
and 3,000,000 more later in Cortina.

His credo is to write as well as he can about things that he knows
and feels deeply about.

The present novel is about love, death, happiness and sorrow. It is

also about the city of Venice and the Veneto, which Hemingway has
known and loved since he was a young boy.

The novel was written in Cortina d'Ampezzo; at Finca Vigia, San
Francisco de Paula, Cuba; and in Paris and Venice.

It is the best novel that Hemingway can write, and he has tried to
make a distillation in it of what he knows about the above subjects
plus one other subject, which is war.

Hemingway is a writer not a soldier, nor has he ever claimed to be
one. His son John, however, is a captain of infantry in Berlin and was
severely wounded, a prisoner after he was wounded and later a
hostage.

To resume answers. You have held me to $25 [cable tolls], so will
omit details of any action or actions that Hemingway has participated
in. His bad knee was acquired by an enemy *Minenwerfer* explosion
which blew off the right knee cap.

Hemingway is bitter about nobody. But the colonel in his book is.
Do you know any non-bitter fighting soldiers or any one who was in
Hürtgen [Forest] to the end who can love the authors of that national
catastrophe which killed off the flower of our fighting men in a stupid
frontal attack?

Hemingway has no opinion in regard to General Eisenhower
except that he is an extremely able administrator and an excellent
politician. H. believes he did a marvelous job in organizing this
invasion, if he was actually the man who organized it. H. means
Hemingway, which I am tired of writing, and *he* in the above
sentence means Eisenhower. Let us revere Eisenhower, Bedell Smith,
the memory of Georgie Patton. But Hemingway refuses to revere
Montgomery as man or soldier, and would rather be stood up against
a wall and shot than make that reverence. He is the gentleman who
took our gasoline to do what he could not do.

Hem admires General Omar Bradley and General Joseph Lawton
Collins and loves the Army of the United States, but cannot love a
chicken division when it is chicken. Love has its limits, but when it is
given it is given for keeps though awful things may happen to it.

In regard to General Dwight D. Eisenhower, Hemingway, catching
another question, only believes that all staff officers should have some
combat experience to be familiar with their tools, which are, or were,
members of the human race. In the last war, Hemingway, a word I'm

getting sick of, was at sea on various projects for approximately two years under the orders of Colonel John Thomason, USMC, Colonel Hayne D. Boyden, USMC, Colonel John Hart, USMC. Then Hemingway left for the ETO and was accredited to the R.A.F. and specifically the tactical air force commanded by Air Marshal "Mary" Coningham. He flew with them for a short time and then was accredited to the Third U.S. Army, from which he escaped while they were waiting around to go. They went very well once the infantry made the hole for them to go through, and held it open on both elbows.

Hemingstein was by this time with an infantry division which he loved [the 4th] and which had three fine regiments, wonderful artillery and good battalion of armor and excellent spare parts. Hemingstein was only a guest of this division, but he tried to make himself useful. He was with them through the Normandy breakthrough, Schnee Eifel, Hürtgen and the defense of Luxembourg.

About the other queries: there are 165,000 words done on the long book [on which Hemingway has been working since 1942]. Thirty thousand words done on poems.

About what he will concede [on the subject of *Across the River and into the Trees*]: we concede nothing, and what we take we hold.

For technicalities, the decorations that Hemingstein the writer holds, and the only ones that he respects, are the *Medaglia d'Argento al Valore Militare* and three *Croce al Merito di Guerra*.

Anything Mary [Mrs. Hemingway] told you over the phone I deny. Every word of this is accurate and true and I vouch for it and you can publish it in full or not at all.

Talk with Mr. Hemingway

Harvey Breit/1950

Reprinted from the *New York Times Book Review* (17 September 1950), 14. Copyright © 1950 by the New York Times Company. Reprinted by permission.

This department has gradually, over a period of seventy-five weeks or so, solidified more or less into a set of conventions. The question is asked, the answer is given; a brief physical description is arrived at; the interlocutor prods, the interlocutee replies by monologue or monosyllable; a brief, very transient sense of the object under surveillance is (it is to be supposed) attained. Let us, then, for this once depart from the conventions. For this week it is Ernest Hemingway who is introduced to the reader, and the tested means are unsuited to presenting that unorthodox, uncompromising figure. The following opinions—some intense, some relaxed, but all profoundly true of Mr. Hemingway— are extracts from a series of exchanges between Mr. Hemingway and this reporter.

On big questions. Honest to God, I don't know the answers to such questions. I am embarrassed by nearly all big pictures—like big questions—except for Tintoretto's "Crucifixion of Our Lord," in Venice. From it I learned principally how to crucify, and how wonderfully the thief on the right behaved. On the right when you look at it. Actually on the left of our Lord.

On Contemporary Themes. That is a lot of deletion. The themes have always been love, lack of it, death and its occasional temporary avoidance which we describe as life, the immortality or lack of immortality of the soul, money, honor and politics. That is an oversimplification. But nobody has employed me to write 150,000 words between covers on any of these themes this morning.

On Country, Culture, Politics, etc. The country that a novelist writes about is the country he knows; and the country that he knows is in his heart. Culture is good to have. It is like a good 1/10,000 map. But you have to make your own attack and remember that no classic resembles another.

We work in our our time; which happens to be the worst time I've ever seen or heard about. But you can have plenty fun in it and still know how bad it is. Politics I would rather not be quoted on. All the contact I have had with it has left me feeling as though I had been drinking out of spittoons. The self-confessed patriot, the traitor and the regulator of other people's lives, beliefs, etc., and the Regimentator all run in a photo-finish. The Senate may develop the picture if they can find a photographer who can photograph a photo-finish. Otherwise they could get a seeing-eye dog. Think it might be a good idea if we could provide all our statesmen and several other characters with such dogs.

On Boxing. Anybody could hit Joe Louis who had the guts to try it. Look at the people who had him down. But he was a good getter-upper. Jack Blackburn could never teach him how not to get hit by left hands. After the first Schmeling fight he taught Louis how to avoid a right. (What you learn in kindergarten.) But Louis hit so hard and beautifully with both hands, he never learned to box.

If you fight a great left-hooker, sooner or later he will knock you on your deletion. He will get the left out where you can't see it, and in it comes like a brick. Life is the greatest left-hooker so far, although many say it was Charley White of Chicago.

On Poetry. Well, I guess some of us write and some of us pitch, but so far there isn't any law a man has to go and see *The Cocktail Party*, by T. S. Eliot from St. Louis, where Yogi Berra comes from. A damned good poet and a fair critic, but he would not have existed except for dear old Ezra, the lovely poet and stupid traitor.

Be a good boy and keep on writing those pieces and maybe they will let you interview the Robert Brownings and the Leigh Hunts and if ever you need relief that will be me you will see moving in from the bullpen with the sorest arm in the world.

On the Novel. Sure, they can say anything about nothing happening in *Across the River,* but all that happens is the defense of the lower Piave, the breakthrough in Normandy, the taking of Paris and the destruction of the 22d Inf. Reg. in Hurtgen forest plus a man who loves a girl and dies.

Only it is all done with three-cushion shots. In the last one I had the straight narrative: Sordo on the hill for keeps; Jordan killing the cavalryman; the village; a full-scale attack presented as they go; and the unfortunate incident at the bridge.

Should I repeat myself? I don't think so. You have to repeat yourself again and again as a man but you should not do so as a writer.

In writing I have moved through arithmetic, through plane geometry and algebra, and now I am in calculus. If they don't understand that, to hell with them. I won't be sad and I will not read what they say. They say? What do they say? Let them say.

Who the hell wants fame over a week-end? All I want is to write well.

Important Authors of the Fall, Speaking for Themselves

Ernest Hemingway/1950

My biographical data is in *Who's Who*. Am a resident of Finga Vigia— San Francisco de Paula—Cuba. About working: I work wherever I am and the earliest part of the morning is the best for me. I wake always at first light and get up and start working. There is a Springer Spaniel from Ketchum, Idaho named Black Dog who helps me to work. Three cats named Boise, Friendless's Brother, and Ecstasy give valuable aid. A cat named Princessa, a smoke-grey Persian, helped me very much; but she died three weeks ago. I do not know what I will do if anything happens to Black Dog or to Boise; just go on working I suppose.

When I finish work I like to take a drink and go swimming. If I have worked well in the morning I try to get out fishing on the Gulf Stream in the afternoon.

In the old days I could read anything. But now I cannot read detective stories any more unless they are written by Raymond Chandler. Mostly I read biography, accounts of voyages that seem true, and military writing, good and bad. You learn about as much from one as from the other.

Fiction has been hard to read lately but I read it. Hope it will be a better year this fall.

Also read the *Morning Telegraph,* when it is obtainable, the *New York Times* and *Herald Tribune.*

Also read three French magazines that I subscribe to, some Italian weeklies, and a Mexican publication called *Cancha* devoted to Jai-Alai. Read the bull fight papers whenever some friend sends them. Read *Harpers, The Atlantic, Holiday, Field and Stream, Sports Afield, True, Time, Newsweek,* and the *Southern Jesuit.* Read *Sat.*

Eve. Post whenever it has a serial by Ernest W. Haycox. Read a
couple or more of Cuban newspapers a day and various South
American literary magazines. Also read *Sport and Country* (British)
and *The Field* (British), also any French books Sartre sends me. Read
several books in Italian each year, some in manuscript and try to get
the ones I believe in published.

Then there is correspondence: I write regularly to a general officer
in the regular army and also to a former Lieut. Gen. in the British
Army whom I knew when we were both young together in Italy. Also
write regularly to about three friends. The rest of the correspondence
is mostly casual or duty or business.

I don't play except for keeps.

Mary has masons, plasterers and painters in the house and I'm
staying at sea until it's over. Also am supposed to be convalescing
from a bad spill I had on the flying bridge, wet deck and very heavy
sea, and my mate just swung her into the trough as I came over the
rail. Got a five inch cut on the back of my head that went into the
bone, a concussion, etc. Severed the artery and it took about five or
six hours before we could get surgical treatment. Luckily Roberto
Herrerra, an old friend, was running behind us. He has had five years
of medicine and he and Mary contained the hemorrhage very well
and his brother José Luis fixed it up.

All it amounts to is that I can't ski this year again. But can swim
and walk and shoot and fish and work although José Luis told me
not to.

But I am getting tired of getting hit on the head. There were 3 bad
ones in '44–'45. Two in '43 and the others go back to '18. People
think they come from carelessness. But they don't. At least none that
I remember did.

Success, It's Wonderful!

Ernest Hemingway/1950

After I have written a book I only wish to see it published exactly as I wrote it and have as many people read it as possible. You write for yourself and for others. This last book [*Across the River and Into the Trees*] was written for people, too, who had lived and would die and be capable of knowing the difference between those two states. It was also written for all people who had ever fought or would be capable of fighting or interested in it. It was written, as well, for people who had ever been in love or were capable of that happiness.

The fact that many people read the book of their own accord and that it is not a packaged product made me very happy. It has not, however, altered my way of life or any plans I may have. I hope to write as well as I can as long as I live. And I hope now to live quite a long time.

Many times critics do not understand a work when a writer tries for something he has not attempted before. But eventually they get abreast of it. The critic, out on a limb, is more fun to see than a mountain lion. The critic gets paid for it so it is much more just that he should be out on that limb than the poor cat who does it for nothing. Altogether I believe it has been quite healthy and the extremely dull thuds one hears as the critics fall from their limbs when the tree is shaken slightly may presage a more decent era in criticism—when books are read and criticized, rather than personalities attacked.

A Letter from Hemingway

Ernest Hemingway/1952

Reprinted from *The Saturday Review*, 35 (6 September 1952), 11.

August 17, 1952

Dear Mr. Kalb:*

Your letter came this morning and today is Sunday. Your deadline is Wednesday. So this may be worthless to you.

Let's skip the clippings. There will be new ones now. Anyway, for better or for worse, you wouldn't want a man to believe his own clippings would you? He would certainly get confused over a period of thirty-four years.

Four hundred words are a lot of words on a Sunday morning unless you are delivering the sermon. Maybe we better put this in question and answer form.

Question: How is the writing going?

Answer: About the same as always. Some days better than others. I've worked two and a half years steady now and could use a vacation.

Question: How is the big book?

Answer: Very long. I am in no hurry about it.

Question: When may we expect it?

Answer: As and when it seems best to publish it.

Question: Do you mean your answers to be curt?

Answer: No, truly. I do not like to talk about my work when I am writing it. Some people do. But, unfortunately, I don't.

Question: How is the fishing?

Answer: It was very good through Spring and early summer. It was worthless during the time of the sun spots and is picking up again now with a very heavy current in the Gulf Stream. We've caught

*Bernard Kalb had written Hemingway for a statement to accompany the cover story on *The Old Man and the Sea*—MJB.

66

twenty-five marlin this season and should get quite a few more. The best year I ever had we caught fifty-four. The fish that are running now are very big. I work in the early morning and fish when I've finished work.

These are all the questions you asked, Mr. Kalb, and we are pretty short on the four hundred words. Would it be any use to know that it has been pleasant and cool here at the farm all summer?

(We had our heat-wave last year.)

The other night it was so cool coming in from the Gulf Stream that I had to put on a flannel shirt and last night I put on a sweater steering home. Mary, my wife, is very well. She loves the ocean and has never been sea-sick and she fishes beautifully. She sleeps in the morning while I wake and work early and she handles all the problems, when she wakes, that I neglect because my head is in the writing. She reads what I write most days and I can tell if it moves her if it gives her gooseflesh. She can't simulate gooseflesh. Now I had better knock-off writing this and write something else.

Good luck.
Yours always,
Ernest Hemingway.

Talk with Ernest Hemingway

Harvey Breit/1952

Reprinted from the *New York Times Book Review* (7 September 1952), 20. Copyright © 1952 by the New York Times Company. Reprinted by permission.

This week Mr. Ernest Hemingway is the news truly. Not only the literary news. Like Earl Sande booting home a Derby winner, or Johnny Vander Meer pitching two no-hitters in succession, or the Manassa Mauler battering big Jess Willard, a book by Papa is front-page news. This fact creates certain misunderstandings. Mr. Hemingway seems to be in the news more than he actually is only because each time he makes his move it starts talk. This is not his fault, and the people who think of Mr. Hemingway as a chap who likes moving into the spotlight are not less than dead wrong. As a matter of record, it would be difficult to find a writer who lives more privately, minding his own business and cultivating his own garden (in the best Voltairean sense of the phrase).

Well, here we are too, just as meddlesome as the rest. Mr. Hemingway writes a small, fine novel, *The Old Man and the Sea,* and instead of letting him be, and being happy about it, we're after him—and there is no discharge from the war. True, we went after him equivocally, ridden by a guilt sufficient to prevent us from asking questions. We merely asked him for a statement, or a number of statements, on whatever was occupying him at the time. Pro and gallant that he is, Mr. Hemingway kicked through with a set of answers to a set of questions that he himself devised. Without further ado, then, here is Mr. Hemingway answering Mr. Hemingway:

Q. How do you feel, Mr. H?

A. Very well, thank you.

Q. What are your plans?

A. To take a vacation, if I have any money left after taxes, and then go back to work.

Q. Where would you like to take your vacation?

A. Either out west or in Europe.

Q. Do you enjoy writing, Mr. H?

A. Very much. But if you do it as well as you can each day, it is tiring.

Q. Do you mind talking about it?

A. I do not believe in talking about it and I try to avoid talking about it. If I have to talk about a book that I have written it destroys the pleasure I have from writing it. If the writing is any good everything there is to say has been conveyed to the reader.

Q. What about fishing?

A. I have enjoyed it ever since I can remember. But I do not enjoy talking about it except to professional fishermen. One of the reasons I quit fishing at Bimini was to avoid the nightly post mortems of the anglers. Another was because the big fish caught were wasted. No fish caught in Cuba is wasted.

Q. Do you spend much time on the sea?

A. In twenty years of my life probably half of it has been spent on the sea.

Q. Can you work while at sea?

A. Perhaps better than anywhere else. My boat, The Pilar,* has no radio, no telephone and, since the war, no radio communications of any kind. You can anchor in the lee of some bay in the Gulf Stream and write on a writing board with no intrusions and you have no excuses if you fail to work well.

Q. Does your wife like the sea?

A. She loves it very much. She has never been seasick and she loves to swim and fish, ·all kinds of fishing, and to watch the stars at night.

Q. Do you have a happy life, Mr. Hemingway?

A. I have never heard a happy life defined. I have always been happy when I am working. If I cannot work I usually do something bad and have remorse and then my conscience makes me work. A conscience tells truths that are as uncomfortable as those a compass sometimes shows. Personally I am happy when I work hard and love someone. Since I have done both these things now for a long time I

*The name of the blasphemous and noble-hearted matriarch of *For Whom the Bell Tolls.*

would say I have a happy life. Times have always been bad. But Walter Raleigh wrote very well the night before he climbed the steps to the scaffold erected in the Old Palace yard of Westminster. I see no reason now not to write well because the times are bad both for those who write and those who read.

A Day in Town with Hemingway

Leonard Lyons/1953

Reprinted, by permission, from the *New York Post* (26 June 1953), 26.

I can say I went elephant hunting with Ernest Hemingway. But the truth is they were not real elephants, only paper targets and our African plain was a Madison Av. shooting range. The gun was real, and the only casualty was a Lyons. Me . . . Let's start from the beginning.

We had breakfast in Leland Hayward's apartment, which the Hemingways were occupying. The manuscript of his new big novel was locked in a bank vault in Havana, and they were leaving for Africa the next day, in search of elephants. Not to shoot them. "I don't like to kill animals," said the man we all call Papa. His wife, Mary, will photograph them and Papa will stand behind her, with his elephant gun, in case the beast should charge.

Hemingway had some old .577 shells and he wanted to test them. We went to Abercrombie & Fitch. He carried the ammo, and I the gun. "If it's heavy, you're out of condition. When its light, you're in shape," he said. He spoke of an offer from a magazine to write a novel on order, for much money. "You can't write a novel to order," he said. "You write it because you must, whether you can sell it or not."

A salesman led us to the basement, and opened a door. It looked like a cement telephone booth. He opened a small metal door, like a safe, and there was the long shooting range. "I was here last with Winston Guest," said Papa. "He was trying out his harpoon gun. He fired it only once, and lost a finger." He cleaned his eyeglasses. "Bad eyes," he said. "Your eyesight gets burned from the rays off the sea." He loaded the double-barreled gun. The shells are big ones. He once had hunted in Africa with Alfred Gwynne Vanderbilt, who brought only 10 of these .577 shells and said: "I didn't bring more because they cost so much."

Hemingway braced himself, and fired. The salesman covered his ears, against the blast. "You don't fire until it's 20 feet away," Papa said about the elephant. "Shoot lions at 100 yards, because a lion can cover 100 yards in 3¾ seconds. You've got to break bone. If you gut-shoot a lion, it won't stop him. You've got to shoot like a surgeon, to break bone."

He gave me the big gun, and warned me to brace myself against the recoil. I did, and aimed and fired. Nothing happened. A dud. "Better it happened here, than in Africa," said Hemingway. The second barrel. This time I forgot to brace myself, and the recoil hurled me against the back of the cement booth and the gun fell from my hand. "You okay?" the salesman asked. Only a wrenched shoulder. "Lucky," he said. "They usually break a collar-bone." Hemingway laughed. "Believe me, the animal would feel worse."

We went upstairs. On the train to N.Y. he had sneezed—and his belt burst. He bought a new one, 40 waist. "Used to be 48 chest, 38 waist," he said. He bought a pistol: "Good around camp, for small game, friends and intruders." He spoke of deep-sea fishing: "Watch the boat vibration. If you can hear it then the fish can hear and won't come up. That's the only trick."

We walked to the Guaranty Trust, to put his trust accounts in order. "Never yet sold a share of stock I bought," he said. "Never had to. I can ride out any depression, as long as they put me in a chair and give me pen and paper." When all the banks closed in '33, he had withdrawn $30,000 and kept the cash in his pocket, "to discipline myself." He offered money to Dorothy Parker and Benchley. But they laughed at him and didn't think the money was real.

He signed his income tax checks. "That estimated tax business. How can any writer estimate his sales?" he said. He began to sign the express checks, and said of his long name, "I was over-named." His check signature differs from his book signature, to make forgery difficult.

We lunched at Shor's, and Toots said of his *Old Man and the Sea:* "Great book. I read it. And if I can read it, anybody can." Toots told of the hand-kissing lesson Papa once gave him: "Simple. You take their hand like this, but don't throw 'em off balance." Toots also told of Hemingway and Hugh Casey, the late Dodger pitcher, trading blows while standing in an open doorway in Havana. A knockdown every punch. Papa won. He never even lost a tooth. "Spitting teeth is for suckers," he said.

Jimmy Cannon joined the table. "In shooting," he said to Cannon, "you got to be careful. Not worried. Great difference between being careful and being worried. Take the cockroach. He goes to the kitchen, eats and doesn't worry." Cannon dissented: "If he were in this restaurant, he'd worry all right." Worry brought mention of the Mau Maus, in the place where Hemingway will stay. "Out of 28,000 whites—18 dead, in two years," said Hemingway. "Give up a country for that?"

Dinner was at the Colony, with the Haywards and Spencer Tracy, who will play the "Old Man" in the movie. They'd taken Tracy to the fishermen in Cuba, who accepted him without knowing he was a movie star. George Jessel came from a nearby table. "You stole your plot from my Uncle Max," he told Hemingway. "His story was called 'Old Max and the Lake.' "

We went to the Cub Room. "Mary and I have so much fun, it's almost as if it were sinful," he said. Johnnie Ray sent a note asking for his autograph. Hemingway signed. He spoke of Cuba, and the fighting cocks he raises. "We got 17 wins and four losses. Sure it's good. Like a pitcher's average. Cruel? What else does a fighting cock like to do?"

He hailed a cab. Sutton Pl. South, he told the driver, then spoke some words in italian. "You an Italian boy? the driver asked, and he said he was from north of Venice. The hackie asked: "Then what are you doing on Sutton Pl. South?"

Doin' good," said Ernest Hemingway. "Doin' pretty good."

Hemingways Survive Two Plane Crackups

Washington Post/1954

Reprinted from the *Washington Post* (26 January 1954), 1.
Reprinted with permission of United Press International, Inc.

Entebbe, Uganda, Jan. 25, UP—Ernest Hemingway arrived here today clutching a bunch of bananas and a bottle of gin after surviving two plane crashes in the elephant country of Uganda.

His head was bandaged and his arm was injured but the celebrated American author quipped: "My luck—she is running very good."

With him was his wife, Mary. She had two cracked ribs and was limping as the 55-year-old Hemingway helped her tenderly from an automobile that brought them here from Butiaba, 170 miles away.

Although he declined an offer to fly out of the jungles right after his second crash yesterday, Hemingway said he will fly again as soon as he finds another plane.

He waves a swollen arm, wrapped in a torn shirt, and appeared to be in high spirits as he brushed aside the near tragic crashes.

He joshed his wife, saying her snoring attracted elephants as they camped overnight near the wreckage of the first plane that crash-landed Saturday near Murchison Falls on the upper Nile.

"We held our breaths about two hours while an elephant 12 paces away was silhouetted in the moonlight, listening to my wife's snores," Hemingway roared.

Mrs. Hemingway, the former war correspondent Mary Welsh of Chicago, smiled.

"And when we woke her," Hemingway said with a wave of the gin bottle, "she said 'I never snore. You've got a fixation about it.'"

"I replied, 'So has the elephant.'"

Hemingway then gave his imitation of the howl of a wild dog to illustrate how he "talked" with the animals that poked around their campfire in the wilds Saturday night.

"Every animal detests the wild dog," he explained. "When you howl all the animals answer, then you know where they are."

Hemingway, who has lived as dangerously as the heroes of his staccato fiction, was examined by a doctor at Butiaba, scene of the second plane crash. An X-ray was advised but he apparently was not badly hurt.

The first crash occurred when a Cessna, piloted by Roy Marsh, cracked up near the 400-foot falls while making an emergency landing.

The second occurred Sunday after the Hemingways hitchhiked by tourist steamer down the Nile to Butiaba. That plane, piloted by T. R. Cartwright, groundlooped into a sisal plantation and caught fire.

Hemingway said the single-engined Cessna they had hired for the flight to Murchison Falls crashed when Pilot Marsh dived at low altitude to avoid hitting a flying flock of ibises—black and white jungle birds big enough to smash the canopy.

Hemingway said that in order to miss the ibises the plane had to land either on a sandspit where six crocodiles lay basking in the sun, or on an elephant track through thick scrub.

Marsh chose the scrub and pancaked the plane in with minor damage. They spent Saturday night around a campfire surrounded by the elephant herd—listening to Mrs. Hemingway's snores—and caught a ride yesterday morning with the launch full of tourists back to Butiaba on Lake Albert.

When the second plane ground-looped and caught fire Hemingway said he butted open the rear door and scrambled out. His wife and the pilot also escaped, but all their luggage was destroyed.

Even when the first crash stranded them overnight in the jungle, Hemingway said he wasn't worried.

"We had emergency goods, but were short on water," he said.

"We took turns going to the river but the elephants were very stuffy about it.

"There were lots of hippos and crocs wandering around the river bank."

Cartwright, who flew here from Butiaba, brought out the first details of the two crashes. He said that when he asked Hemingway about his adventures, the novelist merely replied that he was "very impressed by the wealth of big game."

The Hemingways found big brush fires burning near the edge of the Nile when they first landed and set backfires to save themselves and the plane, Cartwright said.

At twilight they were forced to move back from the banks of the Nile, tormented by swarms of mosquitoes.

For the past few weeks Hemingway and his wife have been on a safari on which he is writing a series of articles for *Look* magazine.

He said he plans to write a book about his current African trip. He said before he began the trip he already had written manuscripts for three books, but hadn't decided when to turn them over to his publishers.

The Sun Also Rises in Stockholm

Harvey Breit/1954

Reprinted from the *New York Times Book Review* (7 November 1954), 1. Copyright © 1954 by the New York Times Company. Reprinted by permission.

In Havana, on Oct. 28, the weather was calm and pleasant. No threat of hurricanes on that day, but plenty of people milling around Finca Vigia, Ernest Hemingway's home outside the capital of Cuba. Two hours before talking to him on the telephone, the news had come officially from Stockholm that Hemingway had won the Nobel Prize. Days before, the rumors had begun and the press was alerted and present.

Now he was on the phone. Over it came noise: agitated sea voices. He sounded neither enthusiastic nor indifferent. He sounded in dead control, and his voice was slow and distinct and careful. There were shouts and low-voiced conversations, coming apparently from behind his back. But he was patient, and his attitude was "go ahead and shoot." He was ready to talk.

About writing Hemingway said: "What a writer must try to do is to write as truly as he can. For a writer of fiction has to invent out of what he knows in order to make something not photographic, or naturalistic, or realistic, which will be something entirely new and invented out of his own knowledge.

"What a writer should try to do is to make something which will be so written that it will become a part of the experience of those who read him."

And criticism: "I have learned very much from criticism when it was of a simple nature. When criticism described me as arrogant, proud or attributed to me other venial sins, I did not learn. I believe that critics know very little about the alchemy of the production of literature. I believe the microphone is one of the greatest enemies of literature, of letters, and that a man should try to imply or show in his written words what he believes, rather than put it into speeches or discourses."

He was reminded that the Italian writer Ignazio Silone once had been asked what was the most important date in history, and that Silone had answered, "the twenty-fifth of December, Year Zero." Hemingway replied, "I have no important dates. And I have never believed in astrology nor in any of the occult sciences. I do not know what Man (with a capital M) means. I do know what a man (small m) is. I do know what man (with a small m) means and I hope I have learned something about men (small m) and something about women and something about animals."

What was he working on now?

With patience and exactness, Hemingway said, "I started to write three short stories about Africa for the collection of stories that Charles Scribner's are planning to publish. There are some seven unpublished stories. I wrote the first story and then when I was well into the second, it started to be a novel. I am writing on this story now—I am writing on this now and it is, as always, both bad and difficult' to discuss what you are writing."

And finally: "As a Nobel Prize winner I cannot but regret that the award was never given to Mark Twain, nor to Henry James, speaking only of my own countrymen. Greater writers than these also did not receive the prize.

"I would have been happy—happier—today if the prize had gone to that beautiful writer Isak Dinesen, or to Bernard Berenson, who has devoted a lifetime to the most lucid and best writing on painting that has been produced, and I would have been most happy to know that the prize had been awarded to Carl Sandburg.

"Since I am not in a position to—no—since I respect and honor the decision of the Swedish Academy, I should not make any such observation. Anyone receiving an honor must receive it in humility."

Though Hemingway is only 55, the prize—highest in value and most distinguished in honor—has been a long time coming. From the beginning, in 1924, when Hemingway published a collection of stories called *In Our Time,* it was apparent that a remarkable and an original talent had entered our life and letters. Any question as to his formidable gifts and art and discipline became idle when, two years later, Hemingway published his first big novel, *The Sun Also Rises.*

He became the most influential and most imitated writer. He dared deal (without saying so in speech or discourse) with what Faulkner has called "the eternal verities of the heart." Passion and wit, brutality and love, lust and ethical concern, action and morality all found their substantial shapes in Hemingway's terse, quintessential and yet (paradoxically) natural language.

What he wrote did become a part of the experience of those who read him. What Hemingway has attempted throughout his career (throughout his life) was no esthetic end so much as a metaphysical one: every clear, strong, crisp word seemed to give expression to the basic attitudes he has held toward all life—so that what one received from him was not a fragment of art so much as the totality of his being. It was concealed, of course, by the best and most natural craftsman of our time. But it was there. One experienced a man engaged with all his seriousness in the serious business of discovering the secrets of life and living. One got it from Balzac in that way, too; in a more intellectual way from Stendhal; and in a more oblique way from Henry James.

A serious writer is, after all, a medium. He himself is the medium. Everything that happens to such a writer, everything that is usable that he experiences—sees, smells, hears, notes—finds its true shape through that medium. So that it could be imagined that what "happened" to Chekhov became short stories at the instant they entered Chekhov's life; or to Yeats, poems; or to Gide, exquisite entries into journals (that is, essentially shapeless).

What results if the serious writer is an artist is a work of real power, because the work is relentlessly honest and relentlessly and intransigently the expression of one's own self. Hemingway's art has had this impact of life, but without the verbiage of art or the muddle of life. It was true from the beginning.

Why then did the "official" recognition come so belatedly? Aside from factors that one can only guess at, each generation takes what it needs, or thinks it wants—and to my mind a crucial job of criticism is precisely to discern what each generation needs. One read *The Sun Also Rises,* and took from it the running of the bulls, the fight between boxer and torero, the cruelty of Brett. One took from *Death in the Afternoon* the eulogy of violence.

What has happened now is that we are reading Hemingway with

greater balance, discovering freshly the beauty of the pastoral in those fishing scenes of *The Sun Also Rises,* the brief and charming relations between American and Spaniard, the moral concern of Brett. In *Death in the Afternoon* one finds the eulogy of valor. Certain events, foreground for another generation, recede for ours, and backgrounds come forward. The humanity and compassion and humility are now established in Hemingway's world as much as conflict and death and violence were for another.

Such readings in the text have obviously seeped down (or up) to the authorities who make momentous decisions. This "timelag" is not necessarily regrettable, though terrible oversights are made during one's lifetime. Joyce did not get a Nobel Prize; Yeats did.

Happily, Hemingway has lived a long time in his short life and he has survived much, including the factions, the critics and the officials. He has lived long enough to see many changes. Year after year, when the prize was awarded to lesser writers, or to less influential writers, Hemingway never complained. He was always gracious. He does not complain now either.

A Journey to Hemingway

Robert Harling/1954

Reprinted, by permission, from the *London Sunday Times* (19 December 1954), 10.

You leave the coast road just outside Havana, and take the Central Highway, going east towards Mantanzas, between the factories, dumps and warehouses. Everything moves fast out here, the shiny Chevs and Cadillacs, even the antique buses.

Soon the shacks and open shops begin. Dirt lanes quit the Highway, struggling vaguely into the low and scrubby hills. Cubans and Negroes, the men in groups, the women alone, sit under the ramshackle porches, play their dominoes or stare.

San Francisco de Paula says the cable I carry like a password in my pocket. Eight miles out of Havana says the map. Then, after a last inquiry at a village store and a sudden swing uphill, the house, or at least its white, defensive palings, marks journey's end.

The carriage gate is padlocked. The ill-drawn lettering on the notice-board is also uninviting. Even I can understand:

SE PROHIBE

ENTRAR

TERMINANTEMENTE

SIN FREVIA

AUDENCIA

POR TELF

But the wicket gates on either side are open and I let myself in. The house is unseen amongst the palm and mango trees. The drive climbs steadily and then sweeps round towards a low white house set above tiled steps.

A firm tap on the wired front door, but no answer. Another tap and the quiet house comes alive with a growl from a bulky figure moving within the room above and the sudden opening of the door by a boy in white.

Hemingway is a big man, even vast. Not more than six feet one or two, perhaps, but built like one of his formidable bulls. That afternoon he was dressed in a blue check shirt, yellow zippered suede waistcoat and dark blue shorts. No socks, no shoes, no sandals.

"You had quite a way to come," he says quietly. "I didn't expect you to be here on time. I would have changed."

But, silently, I doubt it. In any case, the garb becomes him. He has an unusual voice for an American, a burring mumble which at first threatens to be difficult to catch; but every word comes clear and the listener soon relaxes. It is a voice to reconcile the English and American tongues.

The living-room is high and large and comfortable, with white walls and bookshelves, and books, books, books. On one wall is a Spanish bull-fighting poster; in one corner a small, long-playing gramophone precariously balanced on bookshelves; in yet another corner a curved magazine rack, as crowded as a railway bookstall: *Colliers, Life, The Field, The New Statesman,* even, improbably, *The Tatler.*

In the middle of the room are a large sofa and two large armchairs, covered in red-and-white *toile de jouy.* The room is restful, colourful and plainly one man's well-loved home.

We sit down in the two armchairs set side by side, a table between, and begin to talk. The armchairs were made for him. Mine engulfs me like an upturned carapace.

The face, seen in so many photographs, is kinder than any picture ever printed. The beard is white, well trimmed, but still abundant, and seems a natural growth for him, not the affectation of an odd man out. Yet it is not the snowy beard that gives the face its kindliness. Ultimately only the eyes do that for any man. His are brown and benign, and smile frequently behind the pale-grey horn-rimmed spectacles. Sitting there in the big armchair he looks more like a wise and jovial friar than the legendary tough-guy of literature.

I mention the legend, which I never fully believed, and now say so. He smiles and takes up the subject almost eagerly. "Journalists make these legends. They are always in a hurry. They don't always report what one says, but what they want one to say. They want to go on believing certain things about me, so they write them. They even write them before they meet me. One of them even wrote the other day that I gave myself only another five years to live. That's crazy. What I really said was that I'd trade five years of my life to write a good book. That's quite a difference, isn't it? But it's easier for them to write like that than find out that I'm a serious writer."

He smiles. "I'm even a serious man." A pause. "But not a solemn one, I hope."

This hangover of the tough-guy, playboy legend from the thirties into his middle-age (he is fifty-five, but looks older) seems to bother him. He comes back to it. "You know," he says, talking about his African plane crashes, "one German newspaper even suggested I was trying to land the first plane on the summit of Kilimanjaro. As if I were the pilot. As if my wife weren't on board. As if I weren't doing a serious job. After you've travelled a certain number of miles by air you begin to get into the zone for accidents. The law of averages. I'd got into the zone. That's all."

He speaks without rancour of that sense of persecution which sometimes afflicts public figures when talking of the Press.

When does he write?

"In the early morning. Much of my life has been lived in the early mornings. You get going early for hunting or fishing and get into the habit. In any case, my eyelids are thin, I'm told, and it's better for them in the morning. I get up around six, six-thirty, and start work— or try to—by eight. I work until ten-thirty, perhaps even midday. Then the day's my own. I can forget work."

"Even the characters you've been writing about?"

"Put 'em right out of my mind. I must—if they're to come alive again the next day. Every writer has his own way of working. That's mine. I take a drink before dinner. Afterwards I try not to. That can spoil things. Then, through the night, through sleep, the subconscious works with the characters. They're alive again in the morning. You understand? Ready for work."

He goes on to speak about his work. The words come slowly. He seeks for the simplest phrases. "I get embarrassed talking about these things," he says at last, adding with a smile: "I'm old but shy."

He talks on or, more correctly perhaps, muses for a while about

the Nobel Prize. Again his hesitancy appears. It is plain that he fears
the phrase, "The Nobel Prize," thinking it might sound too pompous
on his lips. Instead he refers, almost fearfully, to "This Thing."

"They called me from New York to tell me I was to get it," he says.
"I didn't think that was right. I don't think anyone should know about
that kind of thing in advance. Then the journalists came. I don't know
how many. A crowd. I'm not used to that kind of thing. I'm more
used to attacking than accepting. Prizes aren't good for writers."

He smiles as he amends that sweeping statement. "Not more than
once or twice in a lifetime, anyway. Well, they were all here. They
asked me questions. Then they tossed a coin to see who was to use
the phone first. As if every second counted. One had even rented a
storekeeper's phone down in the village."

We move to another high, white room, invisibly divided into
bedroom and workroom, the white bedcover smothered with letters,
patterned like a patch-work quilt.

"All to be answered," he mumbles gloomily. "From friends. But it's
impossible, I think."

On a shelf by the bed is the Royal portable he uses, typing
standing up. Near the bed is one of those collapsible canvas chairs
which interior decorators have borrowed from the Italian desert army
to make a furnishing rage in New York. Here on the bare tiled floor,
the chair seems in its natural habitat.

The desk in the other half of the room is also covered with papers.
"But I know where everything is," he claims defensively, youthful for
a moment. On the wall behind the desk is a Paul Klee drawing. On
the opposite wall is a high coloured rendering of Kilimanjaro. Next
door is a magnificent Miro, also a fine Dutch painting of dead game.
His taste in the graphic arts is truly catholic, and he is casually
knowledgeable about painting: European, American and Cuban.

We wander out on to the terrace, high above the trees. Havana is
far off but near enough. He points out the Capitol building and four
high belching chimneys. "Polluting the whole of Havana," he says
grimly. "When we first came here all this was clear." He moves his
arm in a wide sweep. "But now you can see." Tumble-down shacks
and small dishevelled houses litter the nearby hillside.

His own house was once a blockhouse, part of the defensive

outworks of old Havana. He has added a tower to the building. We walk towards the tower, its base an open room. "Cat house!" Hemingway says succinctly.

"How many?"

"About thirty. Plus seven, eight or nine dogs. All well behaved."

A tom, currently encaged, considers us broodingly but without hostility as we pass his domain and climb the outside stairs.

Hemingway is moving slowly and stiffly. Is he in pain? I ask remembering that he suffered grievously in his plane crashes: fractured skull, broken spine, ruptured kidney.

"Pain's a subject we don't talk about," he says, the tight-lipped man of action momentarily flashing out. He seems to have a schoolboy's preoccupation with physical courage. He lumbers slowly to the topmost step.

Here, in the tower, he has another workroom, starkly aseptic bookshelves, table and chair, no more. But it must be one of the finest writing-rooms in the world—for a craftsman not over-concerned with comfort.

"I like it here," he growls. "Until it rains. Then I go down again."

A catwalk, like the open bridge of a destroyer, tops the tower. The timbered slopes of the estate fall away towards the village. Once again Hemingway looks out towards Havana. "When Tedder was here I showed him this terrain. One of the first commando operations in modern times was fought out round here."

"American?"

"British. When they took Havana in the seventeen-sixties. Infiltrated through the hills here with the fleet keeping the defenders busy from offshore. The only way to do it. Brilliant. Tedder had lectured on the action at your war college. He was very interested to see it all here."

But he forgets commando operations in the excitement of pronouncing that if he ever gets enough money he'll build a water chute from the top of the tower to the swimming pool, glimmering amongst the trees, sixty feet below, thirty yards off. "That'd be a thrill worth having!" he says, chuckling again.

As we descend from the tower a quiet voice calls "Poppa!" from a hidden doorway. The command is gently peremptory. It is amusing, somehow preposterous, to hear, in his own home, the docile title by which this great literary bear is so widely known in Cuba and the States.

Mary Hemingway, his wife, in a stylish blue-and-black striped shirt-blouse and equally Vogue-worthy black slacks, comes from the house. She is small, fastidiously neat, with short, tawny-coloured hair, an almond-shaped face and watchful, gently feline eyes that seem prepared to smile, but not without premeditation and just cause. She is solicitous of her husband's well-being and offers to act as guide round the garden whilst Hemingway goes indoors.

The great gardening problem in Cuba is to seize and hold colour. In England we come too easily by flowers and cannot begin to apprehend the toil and sweat and yearning that goes into the making of a tropical garden. Every shade of sombre green is there, also the lively colours of hibiscus and bougainvillaea, but never the lyrical colours that we come by so easily. Yet the Hemingways have made a beautiful, colourful garden on his hillside.

We went indoors—to tea! My surprise brings laughter. "I was in England for eight years," she says. "One can't live in a country all that time without acquiring some of its habits." She pours tea from a large silver teapot. Hemingway is well back in his armchair by now, looking more than ever the friar, his legs dangling over the side of the chair. Now that he is no longer talking about himself he smiles and speaks out boldly, the mumble apparently gone for good.

This afternoon his favourite subjects are newspapers and news-paper men, writing and writers, war and warriors.

Hemingway has a wide-ranging knowledge of English journalism and regularly reads *The Times* and *Daily Telegraph, The Sunday Times,* and *Punch.* He thinks that the responsible English newspapers cover American news with unusual fairness and detachment. He speaks with enthusiasm of the understanding which the British Press has brought to the story of McCarthy and McCarthyism.

He switches to a current murder trial in Cleveland, which has aroused enormous interest throughout the States, and says how well two young women journalists are covering the trial. A youngish doctor is alleged to have murdered his attractive wife. Colour shots of the dead woman have been thrown on a large screen. The doctor's brother has rushed to fraternal defence. The trial has everything the public clamours for.

"They call these girls sob-sisters in the old-fashioned Hearst tradition," he says, "but they're not. They write well, and when you consider the speed at which they have to tell their tales it's good, very good. A trial like this, with its elements of doubt, is the greatest human story of all. A skilful writer like Raymond Chandler can make a novel out of violence, but it's still a tale. This is the real thing. This Dorothy Kilgallen is a good girl. Don't you think so?"

I agree, having read Miss Kilgallen's pieces in the *Journal-American.*

"Not as good as Rebecca West, maybe," he says. "Nobody's as good as all that. But those girls are damn good."

Unlike many writers Hemingway seems to find it easy to speak well and generously of other writers. Novels by two younger English authors come in for praise: Gerald Hanley's *The Consul at Sunset* and *The Year of the Lion* and Angus Wilson's *Hemlock and After.*

We still talk of English writers as I leave. He says of Sir Winston, "He is a master of the *spoken* word." Some reservation about Sir Winston's written words? Finally, he speaks gently, almost affectionately, of Cyril Connolly and *The Unquiet Grave,* a book I also keep always near to hand.

"He's lazy and writes too little," I comment, echoing the thoughts of ten thousand Englishmen.

"Perhaps that's a good thing, too, sometimes," Hemingway says gently, and quotes from the book—*The only reason for writing is to write a masterpiece.*

He stands by the door above the steps saying good-bye, a vast and kindly figure, as different from the old, worn, tough-guy legend as a man could be. But could a tough-guy pure and simple have proved such a catalytic influence upon his own and a succeeding generation of writers? Now, at this late day, the artist clearly emerges, ousting the fighter and the huntsman.

Going down the drive I think: If he's not careful he'll end as a revered Old Master.

Perhaps life has tamed him or, at least, mellowed him: but his eyes gleam and his voice rises as he talks of fishing out beyond the Cuban

Keys or of the Battle for Paris, and a man who is prepared to trade five years of his life for the chance of writing one good book is surely not yet old.

April 8, 1955 with Hemingway:
Unedited Notes on a Visit to Finca Vigia

Fraser Drew/1970

Reprinted, by permission, from the *Fitzgerald/Hemingway An-nual 1970,* pp. 108–116.

[These notes were scribbled on a pad in Havana's Rancho Boyeros Airport and on a Delta Airlines plane and then typed the same night on a borrowed typewriter in my room at the Hotel Monteleone in New Orleans. I was spending a week in New Orleans en route back to Buffalo State College from a four-day lectureship at Baylor University in Waco. Except for occasional bracketed comments, notes are in their original rough form.]

Letter from Mary Hemingway waiting when I reached Hotel Monteleone on 3 April, suggesting that I come to see them, sending their Havana phone number, saying that they would "be delighted to see me. Ernest says so specifically." I find that I can fly to Havana on Delta Airlines 8:45 Royal Caribe Thursday evening and return on 2:55 to New Orleans Friday afternoon.

Wednesday night I telephone Cotorro 154 and talk with both Hemingways. EH tries to get me to reverse charges on $10 call. They are having guests Friday afternoon but want to see me Friday morning. EH says that I am to go to Ambos Mundos Hotel where he will make reservations for me as his guest and that chauffeur Juan will pick me up there Friday morning at 9:00 and bring me to the Finca.

Plane flight delayed twice Thursday night, finally gets off at 1:30 a.m. CST and reaches Havana shortly before 5:00 EST. Customs procedure uncomplicated except for a woman just ahead of me who is caught smuggling a boxed live rabbit into Cuba, unacceptable behavior I judge from the gestures and the torrents of Spanish [I speak a little French and a little Irish, but no Spanish]. I have no trouble with my almost empty briefcase and climb aboard the one bus headed for the city. I ride it to the last stop, having no luck in

89

communicating my destination to the driver, and then find a cab driver who takes me to the Ambos Mundos.

EH's old friend Manuel Asper, the proprietor, still waiting up, takes me with some ceremony to "Ernest's Room," unchains and unlocks it, admits me to the high-ceilinged room and bath, and opens a casement window. It is now well past 6:00 and I am to be picked up at 9:00. I go to the window and look out at dawn breaking over the old city. To my left is very old Columbus Cathedral, where the remains of the discoverer rested for many years, and straight ahead and to right the very beautiful harbor of the city, with Morro Castle in the distance. A trumpet begins to sound at ten-minute intervals from an army barracks across the harbor. I cannot sleep but watch the old city rouse to life and the first people come out on the streets—an old woman, a squad of soldiers. It is cool but there is promise of a hot day (it did go over 90).

I bathe and shave and am about to dress when the antiquated telephone rings. It is the proprietor, asking that I join him at 8:00 on the roof-garden for breakfast. I go up and look at a breath-taking panorama of the city and sea, while Manolo points out special things and then shows me his magnificent garden with its open-air dining-room. On the roof grow royal palms and flowering shrubs and vines. There is a shrine to the Blessed Virgin with more than one hundred flowers and plants which take their names from her. We have breakfast: a beaker of orange juice, fresh pineapple, hot white rolls, a pot of coffee—no meat because it is Good Friday. Manolo tells me of his long friendship with the Hemingways, how EH wrote *A Farewell to Arms* and some of *Death in the Afternoon* in the room in which I had stayed, how the three Hemingway boys have made the Ambos Mundos their headquarters as they grew up.

At 9:00 Juan arrives and we drive through the city to the suburb of San Francisco de Paula. Traffic heavy because it is Good Friday and people are going to the churches and the beaches. We stop at a small church. Finally we come to the Hemingway finca and the house may be seen, a sprawling white house on a hill with much land around it. Juan unlocks the gate, drives in, relocks, and we drive up a road between rows of grapefruits, avocados, palms, and strange trees which I do not recognize. Mary is on the terrace with a great armful of flowers and comes to greet me. She is most cordial and apologizes that she cannot spend much time with me because of guests who are coming later in the day. EH appears with the gardener (who is a cross between Robinson Jeffers and Gary Cooper in appearance).

EH is a huge man, dressed in khaki shorts and an old shirt, with gray hair and a gray beard and a ruddy complexion. He shakes hands and welcomes me and seems shy at first, as if I, not he, were the important man. He shows me the house. As one enters, the dining room is straight ahead. It has a long table and on the wall to the left hangs Miro's "The Farm." I recognize the Miro and EH is pleased. He is sure that he likes it for he has looked at it across his table for more than twenty years. I like it, too.

The main room is very long and has tables and chairs and bookshelves and the heads of beasts shot by EH, mainly in Africa. I recognize kudu, eland, and think that I recognize oryx and make a mental note to ask about them later. I forget. To the right of the long room is the library with thousands of books in ceiling-high shelves—natural history, military history, modern literature, here and there a Hemingway. These books were in good order once, said EH, and then there were hurricanes and moves and reorganizations and my boys rearranged them all once according to size and color, not subject. Straight ahead of the long room is the one where Hemingway works much of the time. Most of his work he types, standing, on a typewriter which rests on a bookshelf. There are also a bed, a large table covered with books and unanswered correspondence, and everywhere bookshelves and pictures, including a very good Klee which I do not know by name. Out of all these rooms are French doors to terraces.

Mary comes through the long room. She is 46, the magazines say, but does not look 46. She is blonde and slim and very suntanned and very pretty. EH is 55, will be 56 in July, and looks his age because of the beard and the many accidents he has had. He suggests that we go down by the swimming pool and talk—"Mary will be glad to get us out of the house." A servant brings a glass and a bottle of beer to me and another glass to EH containing "something supposed to be good for my insides," and we walk slowly down the hill to a bench and chairs in a grove beside the pool. EH walks slowly and volunteers the information that he is feeling better but has had some trouble. I've gained too much weight, he adds, but if I exercise enough to keep down the weight it's bad for the vertebrae injured in the crash. He had many injuries in that crash in Africa and in the one that followed it.

It is cool down by the water, a large square blue pool, fourteen feet deep. Across from where we sit is an opening in the trees through which we have a long view of Havana and the sea. There is a breeze, but it is a hot day and Cuba has had no rain in weeks so that trees are less green than they should be. Two dogs accompany us and lie down quietly; they are mongrels and seem intelligent and good-tempered. Cats are all over the place. One kitten kept following me and crying, so that I picked him up and carried him during our look at the house. Nearby I see a small green lizard the color of a lime lollipop and translucent and crystalline in appearance. We sit here and talk for more than two hours, although I make one apologetic move to go which is denied, "unless you have to get back into the city for something."

By this time EH is speaking freely and easily and I feel no awe or self-consciousness. He is a very easy person to be with, slow-moving and slow-speaking, and with the gentle manner which sometimes characterizes the large man and the great man. His voice is quiet and low and his laugh, which comes increasingly as we talk, is genuine and quiet, also. He is very kind and modest and unassuming and much impressed that I should "take so much trouble and come so far" just to see him. When I try to speak of my appreciation for his willingness to see me, he interrupts. I am very grateful for your interest and all you have done, he says. There is something which makes me sure that he means what he says. I think at the time that he always means what he says and says what he means.

Did you bring any books for me to sign? he asks, and I admit having a few in my briefcase. I'll be glad to sign them, he continues. It is very difficult to receive books by mail and return them because of customs and postal regulations, but I am happy to sign any that come here with friends. We'll save time for writing in them when we go back up to the house. I feel brief guilt for six books I had sent him several years before and for the six of his own copies that he had sent back with them as an "act of contrition," he had written, for his delay in returning my copies.

So we go on talking and he talks very well. He speaks often of his wife and is worried about her. Was Mary nice to you when you got here? he asks. I know that she wrote you a nice letter. I read it. But she is not feeling well. And she is worried about these people who are coming this afternoon and about my book. Then, too, her father died a few weeks ago in Gulfport. He had a long and painful death and it was very hard for her. She had to go over there often, of course. I want to take her out in the *Pilar* very soon and get her away from everything for a while. She's sore at me right now, he added, but it's because of all these things.

[Here my notes shift, most of the time, from present tense to past. I'm not sure why. Perhaps because in the brief interval between note-writing at Rancho Boyeros and note-writing on the plane the experience moved across the thin line dividing the present from the past. I also seem to be moving into more complete sentences. The English professor taking over again?]

I asked Hemingway if he was troubled by many visitors. I'm always glad to see friends like yourself and my old war friends and hunting friends, he said, but there are a lot of crazies too. There was a student from New Jersey, one of John Ciardi's boys from Rutgers. I try to be good to students but this one wanted to live here. He is going to be a writer and I had to read three of his stories. They were bad stories. I gave him some criticism that pleased him because it was the opposite of what his teacher had told him in New Jersey. EH went on to say that the boy did not have "basic command of the language," which is necessary before one can "try tricks." EH spoke freely of Mary's father who wanted to write, too. He got all sorts of free advice from me but wouldn't take it, of course. Mary wrote a fine story about him in which he appeared very human but not noble enough to suit him. Attitude of friendly humor toward Mary's father, but no superiority or meanness.

We talked of the books written about Hemingway, the critical studies by Baker, Atkins, Young and Fenton. He was inclined to feel that books should not be written about living men. He was amazed at Atkins' writing his book in Khartoum, far from libraries and primary sources; Atkins did not even have some of the Hemingway books about which he wrote and relied on a *New Yorker* article and what

few books he did have. EH did not like Young's book, for the major
thesis was that the Hemingway books derive from trauma, hurts
experienced from Northern Michigan to Northern Italy, and EH
found that silly. EH does admire Baker and Baker's "big book."
Baker is a nice fellow, said Hemingway, but it is a hard book and
makes too much, as so many critics do, of the symbolism. A
digression then on the matter of symbolism—"No good writer ever
prepared his symbols ahead of time and wrote his book about them,
but out of a good book which is true to life symbols may arise and be
profitably explored if not over-emphasized." Back to this later. The
Fenton book he finds over-done. Fenton is a "disappointed creative
writer and a disappointed FBI investigator." He belongs to the
"laundry-list school" of literary criticism, over-investigating and then
over-interpreting. Fenton, for example, over-emphasized the influence of Moise, a *Kansas City Star* editor during EH's apprenticeship
there. Moise was a bad writer who wrote a long poem that he was
always inflicting on people, said EH. It was no good, but how can
you tell an old man his poem is no good?

EH asked about my trip to Baylor and I told him that there was
great interest among the students there in his work, much more than
in the work of Masefield, about whom I had also lectured at Baylor.
EH wanted to know if Masefield was still living. He must be a very
nice guy, he said, and he wrote some good adventure stories as well
as good poems.

Tell me about teaching, Hemingway asked. He wondered why I
had gone into teaching, if I liked it, and if the theme-reading got me
down. It must be hard work, he said, but it is very important. The
corruption of youth is the greatest crime and the good teaching of
youth a temendous responsibility. He then told me that he much
appreciated my teaching of his books. I don't teach them, I said. I
don't have to sell them. I merely suggest them, along with other
books; they always sell themselves and the great majority of students
like them. Which one do they like best, he wanted to know. I
answered that their first choice was probably *A Farewell to Arms.*
When I added that my own favorite was probably *The Sun Also
Rises,* he said that it was the most moral book he had ever written, a
sort of "tract against promiscuity." You don't look like a teacher, EH
said. You have the face of a doctor. He asked if I had ever thought of

being a doctor, and I admitted that I had and told him why I had
become a teacher instead. I like to think that his remarks implied a
compliment, remembering his love for his father, who was a doctor,
and remembering the attractive figure of Rinaldi in *A Farewell to
Arms*. I told EH how much I had liked the Ambos Mundos and
Manuel Asper. He talked of his long residence there and long
friendship with Manolo, but he had not written all of *Farewell* there,
as Manolo believed.

Somehow we got back onto the subject of the critics and literary
criticism, and Hemingway spoke of the great amount of adverse
criticism he had received in recent years, particularly between the
time of much-damned *Across the River and Into the Trees* and the
appearance of the much-hailed *The Old Man and the Sea*. He spoke
of the tendency of critics to over-identify him with the characters of
his books and spoke at some length on the subject in connection with
Jake Barnes of *The Sun Also Rises*. It is true that I got the idea when
I was in the hospital in Italy after I had been wounded, he said. I too
had been wounded in the groin and there had been wool infection
there. I was swollen up like footballs, he gestured dramatically, but I
was not made impotent like Jake Barnes, obviously. I was put into a
so-called genito-urinary ward where there were many guys with groin
wounds, and it was pretty bad. That is where I got the idea for Jake,
not from myself. But of course people thought that he was a self-
portrait. Once, EH said, the photographer Man Ray took a trick nude
picture of him in which a gaping wound appeared in the front of his
body. The picture was apparently shown to a writer-friend whose
wife, not widely celebrated for her good sense, met EH a few weeks
later at a cocktail party. After a few drinks, she suddenly rushed over
to Hemingway, threw her arms around his neck, and cried, "You
poor darling. Now I understand about Jake Barnes and I know what
they mean by a fate worse than death." The laugh was hearty when
he told the story, but there was an edge of exasperation on it.
Continuing with the critics, he commented on their willingness to
publish extravagant theories about people. They've said everything
about me except that I'm homosexual, and that will be the end, and
he laughed again. But he launched into an attack against irresponsible biography and criticism, citing particularly a recent book on
Lawrence of Arabia. The book's presentation of Lawrence's il-

legitimacy and his sexual proclivities infuriated Hemingway, especially since Lawrence's mother and other members of the family were still living.

I spoke of its being Good Friday and recalled Hemingway's early *Today is Friday.* He then asked me if I went to church and I told him that I am a Roman Catholic, though originally a Congregationalist. This interested EH. He said, I like to think that I'm a Catholic, as far as I can be. I can still go to Mass, although many things have happened—the divorces, the marriages. He spoke with admiration of Catholicism and then of his friend, the Basque priest whom he had known in Spain and who now lived in San Francisco de Paula. He comes here a great deal, said EH. He prays for me every day, as I do for him. I can't pray for myself any more. Perhaps it's because in some way I have become hardened. Or perhaps it is because the self becomes less important and others become more important. But that *Time* article was bad. He referred to a recent article in *Time* which had commented that he had been born a Congregationalist, had become a Roman Catholic, and now no longer went to church. This conversation with EH confirms my earlier feeling that he is a religious man with respect for the religions of others.

Now I mentioned the time, fearing that I would complicate his schedule for the rest of the day. He said, Let's go up to the house and sign those books of yours. We walked slowly up the hill to the house, where we saw Mary and I thanked her for putting up with my intrusion. She was very gracious. EH then asked for the books. I had not brought any on my trip from Buffalo, for I had not expected to go to Havana. I wished that I had with me my copies of *Three Stories and Ten Poems* and *in our time,* his first two books. In New Orleans I had ransacked the bookshops for Hemingway firsts as soon as I knew that I was going to Havana, but I had found only one, a second issue of *A Farewell.* This I took along, as well as copies of *A Farewell, The Sun,* and *The Old Man and the Sea* for my three best students at the college, a *To Have and Have Not* for my colleague, Professor Conrad J. Schuck, and an *Old Man and the Sea* for George A. Drew, my father. EH inscribed the books for their recipients, asking for information about each, and also a photograph of himself for me. Then he said, I want to give you two or three other things. He brought back to the table a first issue of *The Spanish Earth,* a book which I did not have in my collection, noting that it was the "author's copy," as well as a first Italian edition of *The Old Man*. These he inscribed, carefully and variously, and then he found an Italian edition of *For Whom the Bell Tolls* and a French edition of *Farewell* and inscribed them. I was delighted to stuff them into the briefcase which had been my only baggage from New Orleans, though wishing now that I had brought a suitcase.

With some inner conflict I declined an invitation to stay for late lunch because the about-to-arrive guests were friends of long standing and I had no wish to intrude upon what might have been an anniversary occasion of the type which my host cherished. We walked out onto the terrace and EH instructed Juan the chauffeur to stay with me for as long as I wanted him that afternoon. He may want to drive around the city and take a later plane from Rancho Boyeros, he said to Juan. Now I want you to come again, he said to me. This has been a pleasure for me and I hope that you are not too badly disappointed after coming so far and taking so much trouble. "Writers are always a disappointment when you meet them. All the good in them goes into their books, and they are dull themselves." I'm sure that I remember these words exactly as he said them. I assured him that he was wrong and that the visit had been all for which I had hoped and more. Next time, he said, give me longer notice and I'll save time for taking you out in the *Pilar* and for showing you the city. And don't call me "Sir," he said, shaking my hand and putting the other great hand on my shoulder. Mary came out again as I was getting into the car with Juan. "Goodbye," she called, "and excuse me for being so busy." "Good luck," called Hemingway, and we drove down to the gate and out onto the road for Havana.

It was blazing hot but Juan's speed gave us good breeze. I watched the houses and people and looked at the harbor and occasional landmarks pointed out by Juan in his very good English. But I kept thinking about the friendliness and the wisdom of the man I had been visiting. At Rancho Boyeros I found that the Royal Caribe from Caracas was very late. I passed the time by writing the first pages of these notes on a pad of paper I had stuffed into the briefcase and by watching arrivals and take-offs of other planes, especially one bound for Buenos Aires and another for Mexico City. There were others for

Miami and Houston and Montego Bay and the airport was crowded and busy. The flight to New Orleans was as smooth as it had been the night before. Was it really only the night before? We flew so high that I could not see the Gulf at all, and I continued writing until we came down over the Mississippi Delta and flew low up the river's winding course for many miles. Then New Orleans Airport, the line-up at Customs and Immigration and Board of Health, and a car back to the Monteleone in time for a shower, a little time in nearby St. Louis Cathedral, and a late dinner in the Quarter.

[Epilogue note, 1970: A 1962 letter from Mary ends, "I am so glad that Papa had time to chat with you that day." So am I, needless to say. It was one of the four or five best days of my life.]

Hemingway Tells of Early Career;
States That He "Won't Quit Now"

Jack Goodman, John Milton, Alan Graber, Bill Tangney/1955

Reprinted, by permission, from the *Daily Princetonian* (14 April 1955), 3.

On April 6, 1955, four sophomore reporters, Jack Goodman, John Milton, Alan Graber and Bill Tangney, interviewed Ernest Hemingway at his Cuban villa, "Finca Vigia." His comments on writing and literature are included in this article.

Papa scratched his ankle and squinted into the hot sun. The brief silence was disturbed only by the distant clamor of fighting cocks and the rumble of road construction in the little town of San Francisco de Paula below Finca Vigia.

We began to talk, leaning over a hewn table by the side of his pool, Hemingway resting heavily on his elbows, speaking gently through the mass of white beard on his face. But at first he was almost incoherent, and he squinted, shook himself once or twice, blinked.

"You'll excuse me," he said with a speech defect at first pronounced and later subdued. "I have been concentrating deeply on my writing; it takes me a while to come back out of it."

He was the last man one would guess had triumphed through countless wounds, two wars and three plane crashes. He talked softly, hands together, looking like a tropical Santa Claus.

The novelist rambled on about an assortment of subjects, ranging from Cuban politics to marlin fishing on his boat "Pilar." But as we settled back with our second round of martinis, Hemingway began recounting his early days as an expatriate writer in Europe.

"I first knew I wanted to be a writer when I was twenty. At that time, I knew I was good, even though all my stuff had been rejected. It was discouraging because all my friends were writing novels and getting them published, and I was having trouble even writing a decent paragraph. I couldn't understand how those guys did it.

"Finally, I got disgusted and knew I was getting old (he was twenty-four) so at Valencia I started my first novel. That was *The Sun Also Rises*. It took me six weeks to write and six months to cut out all the crap."

Hemingway was working at the time as a newspaperman, but here is his opinion of this job: "I hated newspaper work because I was shy and didn't like to ask people questions about their private lives."

To this day Hemingway doesn't like to be interviewed. He likes to talk to people but it's a different matter when there's a pencil and pad waving in his face.

Papa disclosed that one of his most difficult tasks as a young writer was learning to use the third person as a vehicle for telling a story. "I had trouble with the third person and it took me some time to correct it. It's easy to write in the first person, but in the third person you are God and can know everything. I wrote *The Sun Also Rises* in the first person, but I knew I had to write in the third person, too. To practice this method, I wrote *Death in the Afternoon,* but it wasn't until *For Whom the Bell Tolls* that I really caught on."

The subject of conversation turned to his latest novel *The Old Man and the Sea,* which was largely responsible for his recent Nobel Prize in Literature. He said, "The sea is very hard to write about. It is very complex. I thought about *The Old Man and the Sea* for twenty years. I knew I had to write it. When I got into it, everything went right—I had good luck all the way," he added, knocking on the wooden table three times.

We asked him if his repeated mention of Joe DiMaggio would date the book. He looked up and shook his head, saying "Joe DiMaggio is not as dated as Marilyn Monroe. What I was trying to do was to present a true picture of a fisherman, and down here the fishermen are crazy about baseball."

The conversation turned to symbolism in his books. He declared, "I know what I'm writing about but I never throw in symbols consciously. Sometimes I find out what I'm supposed to mean when I read the books on my work. I guess somewhere some of the same ideas must be in me. I certainly do have crazy ideas."

"I have the most fouled-up dreams," he added. "If I told anyone about my dreams I'd be thrown in the looney-bin."

We asked him if a successful writer can "coast" on his reputation. He admitted that it can be done, but emphasized that "Writing is a tough profession. I really work at it. It's tough, but then everything is tough. I enjoy writing while I'm doing it and after I've finished. The worst time is just before."

Asked if he'll ever "run out," he chuckled and said, "I've been going this far. I don't see how I can quit. Why should I stop going the way I am?" He added, "Once a story is written it's out of your system."

Hemingway then turned to his experiences which have left his body covered with numerous scars. We asked him if a writer had to go out and look for experiences, to which he replied, "You can't help having experiences. You don't have to go out looking for them. You don't need crashes in jungles to be able to write stories. I try to avoid experiences like these," he said with a sly grin, "but I'm not always too successful at this."

Referring to the evolution of his writing, he pronounced, "Out of the muck of experience grow the plants," probably recalling the great volumes of muck and great reams of "plants" that have filled his hectic life.

We shook hands with him, downed the remainder of the Martini mix (100-to-1 ratio) and set off down the hill towards San Francisco de Paula. The noise of the screeching fighting cocks grew louder and soon we were winding through the road construction to a little open-air cafe. We ordered nickel shots of Cuban cane-rum and wrote down everything we could remember about the interview. It was dusty and hot in the cafe and we gazed longingly at the villa on the hill overlooking the town.

*On 13 April Hemingway informed Prof. Carlos Baker:**

Those four members of the class of 1957 showed up at the door of the house at eleven a.m. of a morning when I had been trying to

*(Stanford University Library: this letter is facsimiled in Albert J. Guerard, "Hemingway at Stanford." *California* [September 1985].)—MJB

work since 6 a.m. and finally gotten going good about ten thirty. There is a sign on the gate that says visitors received by appointment only in both English and Spanish. But that does not deter anyone nowadays and one of the things considered smartest this Spring Vacation has been for students to crash that gate.

Anyhow since the boys had a letter from you I received them and asked them if they would excuse me while I went on writing (Can you imagine a man having to ask to be forgiven for asking permission of undergraduates to try to continue important work which is being interrupted) and asked them to go down at the pool and swim and I would join them when I was through. Asked René to take them down some beer to the pool. I tried to work some more, finished a paragraph, tried to get going again (I was in the most important part of the book) but my work was upset for keeps so I put on a shirt, asked Rene to get me a glass of coconut water and went down to the pool. There I joked with the boys, made fun of writing, said I just wrote and then you interpreted it, and tried to relax from how sick and awful I felt from having my work bitched. It happened four times in one week. Once the people had gotten into the house I was polite and tried to be friendly. Four different Universities.

Hemingway, "Writing Good," About to Bank Another Book

Earl Wilson/1955

Reprinted, by permission of Earl Wilson and the *New York Post,* from the *New York Post* (9 November 1955), 17.

Havana, Nov. 9—The Ernest Hemingway news is: "Papa is feeling good—and writing good—and about to put another book in the bank."

His wife, Mary Welsh ("Miss Mary" to him), dispelled scary rumors about his health when I visited their farm at San Francisco de Paula. Then he took me to "dinner in town"—a perilous adventure for anybody lacking his vitality.

"I haven't been off the reservation in a week," he said restlessly, his beard looking picturesque.

"Sure, when you're 56, had your back broken, and skull fractured, and kidneys and bladder smashed, you're not your best—but I'm fine. I finished Page 667 today. By February, I may have her done and in the bank."

"In the bank?" I asked.

"I've got three unpublished ones in the bank. This'll be the fourth. I put 'em away and let 'em ripen."

He can always take a book out and cash it. It's Hemingway-type insurance. He hunts wars, sleeps with a gun near his bed and battles half-ton fish—so he'll never be an insurance company pet.

"I was sorry we got people so spooked about our two crashes in Africa," he said. " 'Miss Mary' had never seen a plane burn up before. That's a very impressive sight—especially when you're in the plane."

He remembers an English doctor pouring gin in the crack in his skull and saying, "Laddie, gin is as good for you on the outside as it is on the inside."

"Papa" spoke pridefully of Mary (who looked fresh and youthful in her shorts), of her fishing, of her swimming . . .

103

"She's such a good shot, I must take those shells out of her shotgun!"

Hemingway's gentler and more modest even than before. So as not to sound braggy, the ex-Kansas City courts reporter didn't mention his Nobel Prize by name; he spoke of it quietly as "the Swedish thing . . ."

"Since the Swedish thing, it's chic to crash our gate. We get a lot of crazies and a lot of s.o.b.'s."

"But one night," spoke up Mary, "Papa invited in three sailors waiting at 1 a.m.—and gave them the champagne he'd cooled for us."

About March 1—probably after a trip to Europe—he'll fish off South America for the giant marlin for *The Old Man and the Sea* movie.

"This has to be the fish to end all fish," he said. I asked how big. "Fifteen hundred to 2,000 pounds," he answered.

When we drove into the Floridita, home of frozen daquiris, he waved happily to farmers and tradespeople. A man I thought to be a begger came up. I gave him a quarter. Hemingway thrust it back and gave him a bill.

Inside, I commented how kindly he gave autographs.

"Sure," he said. "What we don't ever want to do is get swellheaded."

McCall's Visits Ernest Hemingway

Kurt Bernheim/1956

Reprinted, by permission of Toni Strassman, from *McCall's*, 83 (May 1956), 6, 8, 10.

The Hemingways live in a Spanish-style farmhouse, by taxi half an hour from Havana City. Their 15-acre estate, Finca Figia (Look-out Farm), is fenced in all around and the main gate carries a sign to keep out trespassers. But the gate swings open for us since Ernest Hemingway had invited us for lunch the day before. Our chauffeur drives up a short, crooked path and with a flourish brings his car to a sudden halt. "There he is," he says, pointing toward a large French door. The outlines of a heavy man are visible behind it; he gives us time to climb halfway up a few steep stairs leading to a stone terrace and to catch our breath before coming out and welcoming us.

At first glance, Ernest Hemingway looks quite different from his photographs. There is no bounce to his gait, no he-mannish bravado. This is a tired man with a sizable paunch, whose military carriage seems to be a matter of discipline and will power rather than strength. He cheers up considerably, however, after settling down in his huge living room on an easy chair and after his "boy" has brought in the first round of (very) dry martinis.

He makes no secret that he loves his profession, "I wish to write and write well. If it weren't so, I would have become a businessman or an engineer long ago, and I might have been more successful at that." Money, honors and success are rather immaterial to him. He would continue writing without them and wouldn't care about publishing either.

He tells us that he has four completed and unpublished novels, however, stacked away safely in the vaults of banks of the United States and Cuba—the actual script in one country and the microfilm in the other. There is nothing wrong with these novels; he likes all of them fine. But since taxes take out a bite of 85 per cent of his total earnings, he just can't afford to have them raised any further. "This is

105

the security I am leaving behind for my family," he says, "and my publishers won't have to worry either." Hemingway doesn't tell what these novels are about; they might very well contain a large work of which *The Old Man and the Sea* is only a part, or a novel on World War II, in which he was actively engaged on land, on sea and in the air.

Only at the luncheon in the spacious dining room does his wife, Mary Hemingway, join us. She is a small woman with a rather boyish figure and a pleasant face, whose only make-up consists of a faint trace of lipstick. The oblong mahogany table, shining in dark splendor, is carefully set for four. The conversation flows freely, without effort and without dead stops, touching lightly on the biographical data of everyone at the table, on American politics, infantry tactics, the little knowledge man can accumulate during a lifetime and the relative merits of the other American Nobel Prize winners in literature. Hemingway says he always knows, Nobel Prize winners or not, where a writer's weak spots are, but "this is a *secret du métier,* a kind of covering-up, as one soldier does for his comrade in battle."

Luncheon is served with the precision of a perfect military drill. Mary Hemingway rings her hand bell, which cuts loudly and demandingly into her husband's low and confidential tone of voice, and instantly, quietly the servant appears with each course. First comes a creamy soup with solid chunks of something in it that tastes like chicken of never-before-experienced delicacy but turns out to be fish—caught and prepared by our hostess; then chicken that looks, smells and tastes like the real thing, roasted to juicy tenderness, with cooked Cuban rice and steamed vegetables; finally, preserves that appear to be green peppers in vinegar but have the flavor of apricots of an unknown, bittersweet kind; and, of course, demitasse—strong Cuban coffee, served with cream and sugar in oversize thimbles.

Mary Hemingway calls herself a housewife. (She was with the London Bureau of *Time* magazine when she met Hemingway in 1944, married him two years later.) "Housewife," in her case, means that she prepares the menus for the master, keeps Finca Figia running smoothly, acts as Hemingway's business manager and confidential secretary and keeps up with him on his adventurous trips. She had never fished before meeting Hemingway, but came within reach of last year's Havana championship. The big fish had already been alongside her own tiny boat, but at the last moment he opened his mouth and spat out the bait. "Good fisherwoman," says Hemingway reassuringly. "Boats them fast."

After luncheon the Hemingways patiently pose for outdoor photographs. Ernest Hemingway takes off his professorial spectacles ("to look less horrible"), and his wife improvises intimate poses against her husband's mild protests. Who can blame her for showing off that hers is the prize catch? She tells us that old Finca Figia was bought by Hemingway in 1939, and that only a studio was added to the simple one-story building.

We walk back into the pleasantly cool house. There is nothing pedantic or pretentious about the interior. The doors leading from one room into the next are kept wide open to let the air circulate freely. In Hemingway's downstairs study, the stuffed head of a ferocious-looking beast stares down from the wall at the master's desk. Books are all over the place, spreading out into every room. Upon a magazine's cabled query, Mary Hemingway has just finished counting the book supply in stock. There are 4,623 volumes around the house, all read with the exception of *Who's Who*. Hemingway occasionally reads three books a day ("keeps me from thinking about my work") and a great variety of magazines ("like some people chew gum"). "The books that sound good" he buys sight unseen and often passes on to friends among the native cattle ranchers and sugar planters.

Mary Hemingway retires for a late siesta, and her husband graciously offers to sit again for the photographer, this time on the stairs where we met him six hours ago. He also answers a few more questions for us.

What does he feel is a woman's role in a man's life?

"A woman should be properly loved as one is able and according to her deserts. Men and women have their duties and pleasures and rewards, also the right to make mistakes if they are not intentional ones."

Any advice for young people who want to become writers?

"Work for it hard and not be disappointed. If they are any good, anybody will tell them for a long time that they aren't any good. Tell them: 'No classic resembles any previous classic, so do not be discouraged.' "

The daylight has faded away, and Ernest Hemingway gets up stiffly.

What is his opinion on the Nobel Prize for Literature? He replies slowly, carefully, making sure that his words are taken down correctly:

"I am very happy for any writer who deserves it to get the prize. I am sorry about any writer who deserves it and doesn't get it. This makes me very humble in accepting it. One shouldn't win the Nobel Prize, then rewrite the *Bible* and become a bore—I accepted the *Bible* in its original version."

The Art of Fiction: Ernest Hemingway

George Plimpton/1958

Reprinted from *The Paris Review*, 5 (Spring 1958), 60–89. Interview with Ernest Hemingway by George Plimpton in *Writers at Work: The Paris Review Interviews*, Second Series, edited by Malcolm Cowley. Copyright © by the Paris Review, Inc. Reprinted by permission of Viking Penguin, Inc.

Hemingway: You go to the races?
Interviewer: Yes, occasionally.
Hemingway: Then you read the *Racing Form*
. . . there you have the true Art of Fiction.

—*Conversation in a Madrid cafe, May, 1954*

Ernest Hemingway writes in the bedroom of his home in the Havana suburb of San Francisco de Paula. He has a special workroom prepared for him in a square tower at the south-west corner of the house, but prefers to work in his bedroom, climbing to the tower-room only when "characters" drive him up there.

The bedroom is on the ground floor and connects with the main room of the house. The door between the two is kept ajar by a heavy volume listing and describing "The World's Aircraft Engines." The bedroom is large, sunny, the windows facing east and south letting in the day's light on white walls and a yellow-tinged tile floor.

The room is divided into two alcoves by a pair of chest-high bookcases that stand out into the room at right angles from opposite walls. A large and low double-bed dominates one section, over-sized slippers and loafers neatly arranged at the foot, the two bedside tables at the head piled seven-high with books. In the other alcove stands a massive flat-top desk with two chairs at either side, its surface an ordered clutter of papers and mementos. Beyond it, at the far end of the room, is an armoire with a leopard skin draped across the top. The other walls are lined with white-painted bookcases from which books overflow to the floor, and are piled on top amongst old

109

newspapers, bullfight journals, and stacks of letters bound together
by rubber bands.

It is on the top of one of these cluttered bookcases—the one
against the wall by the east window and three feet or so from his
bed—that Hemingway has his "work-desk"—a square foot of
cramped area hemmed in by books on one side and on the other by
a newspaper-covered heap of papers, manuscripts, and pamphlets.
There is just enough space left on top of the bookcase for a
typewriter, surmounted by a wooden reading-board, five or six
pencils, and a chunk of copper ore to weight down papers when the
wind blows in from the east window.

A working habit he has had from the beginning, Hemingway
stands when he writes. He stands in a pair of his oversized loafers on
the worn skin of a Lesser Kudu—the typewriter and the reading-
board chest-high opposite him.

When Hemingway starts on a project he always begins with a
pencil, using the reading-board to write on onion-skin typewriter
paper. He keeps a sheaf of the blank paper on a clipboard to the left
of the typewriter, extracting the paper a sheet at a time from under a
metal clip which reads "These Must Be Paid." He places the paper
slantwise on the reading-board, leans against the board with his left
arm, steadying the paper with his hand, and fills the paper with
handwriting which in the years has become larger, more boyish, with
a paucity of punctuation, very few capitals, and often the period
marked with an x. The page completed, he clips it face-down on
another clipboard which he places off to the right of the typewriter.

Hemingway shifts to the typewriter, lifting off the reading-board,
only when the writing is going fast and well, or when the writing is,
for him at least, simple: dialogue, for instance.

He keeps track of his daily progress—"so as not to kid myself"—
on a large chart made out of the side of a cardboard packing case
and set up against the wall under the nose of a mounted gazelle
head. The numbers on the chart showing the daily output of words
differ from 450, 575, 462, 1250, to 512, the higher figures on days
Hemingway puts in extra work so he won't feel guilty spending the
following day fishing on the Gulf Stream.

A man of habit, Hemingway does not use the perfectly suitable
desk in the other alcove. Though it allows more space for writing, it

too has its miscellany: stacks of letters, a stuffed toy lion of the type sold in Broadway nighteries, a small burlap bag full of carnivore teeth, shotgun shells, a shoe-horn, wood carvings of lion, rhino, two zebras, and a wart-hog—these last set in a neat row across the surface of the desk—and, of course, books. You remember books of the room, piled on the desk, bedside tables, jamming the shelves in indiscriminate order—novels, histories, collections of poetry, drama, essays. A look at their titles shows their variety. On the shelf opposite Hemingway's knees as he stands up to his "work-desk" are Virginia Woolf's *The Common Reader,* Ben Ames Williams' *House Divided, The Partisan Reader,* Charles A. Beard's *The Republic,* Tarle's *Napoleon's Invasion of Russia, How Young You Look* by one Peggy Wood, Alden Brook's *Shakespeare and the Dyer's Hand,* Baldwin's *African Hunting,* T. S. Eliot's *Collected Poems,* and two books on General Custer's fall at the battle of the Little Big Horn.

The room, however, for all the disorder sensed at first sight, indicates on inspection an owner who is basically neat but cannot bear to throw anything away—especially if sentimental value is attached. One bookcase top has an odd assortment of mementos: a giraffe made of wood beads, a little cast-iron turtle, tiny models of a locomotive, two jeeps and a Venetian gondola, a toy bear with a key in its back, a monkey carrying a pair of cymbals, a miniature guitar, and a little tin model of a U.S. Navy biplane (one wheel missing) resting awry on a circular straw placemat—the quality of the collection that of the odds-and-ends which turn up in a shoebox at the back of a small boy's closet. It is evident, though, that these tokens have their value, just as three buffalo horns Hemingway keeps in his bedroom have a value dependent not on size but because during the acquiring of them things went badly in the bush which ultimately turned out well. "It cheers me up to look at them," Hemingway says.

Hemingway may admit superstitions of this sort, but he prefers not to talk about them, feeling that whatever value they may have can be talked away. He has much the same attitude about writing. Many times during the making of this interview he stressed that the craft of writing should not be tampered with by an excess of scrutiny—"that though there is one part of writing that is solid and you do it no harm by talking about it, the other is fragile, and if you talk about it, the structure cracks and you have nothing."

As a result, though a wonderful raconteur, a man of rich humor, and possessed of an amazing fund of knowledge on subjects which interest him, Hemingway finds it difficult to talk about writing—not because he has few ideas on the subject, but rather that he feels so strongly that such ideas should remain unexpressed, that to be asked questions on them "spooks" him (to use one of his favorite expressions) to the point where he is almost inarticulate. Many of the replies in this interview he preferred to work out on his reading-board. The occasional waspish tone of the answers is also part of this strong feeling that writing is a private, lonely occupation with no need for witnesses until the final work is done.

This dedication to his art may suggest a personality at odds with the rambunctious, carefree, world-wheeling Hemingway-at-play of popular conception. The point is, though, that Hemingway, while obviously enjoying life, brings an equivalent dedication to everything he does—an outlook that is essentially serious, with a horror of the inaccurate, the fraudulent, the deceptive, the half-baked.

Nowhere is the dedication he gives his art more evident than in the yellowtiled bedroom—where early in the morning Hemingway gets up to stand in absolute concentration in front of his reading-board, moving only to shift weight from one foot to another, perspiring heavily when the work is going well, excited as a boy, fretful, miserable when the artistic touch momentarily vanishes—slave of a self-imposed discipline which lasts until about noon when he takes a knotted walking stick and leaves the house for the swimming pool where he takes his daily half-mile swim.

Interviewer: Are these hours during the actual process of writing pleasurable?

Hemingway: Very.

Interviewer: Could you say something of this process? When do you work? Do you keep to a strict schedule?

Hemingway: When I am working on a book or a story I write every morning as soon after first light as possible. There is no one to disturb you and it is cool or cold and you come to your work and warm as you write. You read what you have written and, as you always stop when you know what is going to happen next, you go on from there. You write until you come to a place where you still have your juice and know what will happen next and you stop and try to live through until the next day when you hit it again. You have started at six in the morning, say, and may go on until noon or be through before that. When you stop you are as empty, and at the same time never empty but filling, as when you have made love to someone you love. Nothing can hurt you, nothing can happen, nothing means anything until the next day when you do it again. It is the wait until the next day that is hard to get through.

Interviewer: Can you dismiss from your mind whatever project you're on when you're away from the typewriter?

Hemingway: Of course. But it takes discipline to do it and this discipline is acquired. It has to be.

Interviewer: Do you do any re-writing as you read up to the place you left off the day before? Or does that come later, when the whole is finished?

Hemingway: I always re-write each day up to the point where I stopped. When it is all finished, naturally you go over it. You get another chance to correct and re-write when someone else types it, and you see it clean in type. The last chance is in the proofs. You're grateful for these different chances.

Interviewer: How much re-writing do you do?

Hemingway: It depends. I re-wrote the ending to *Farewell to Arms,* the last page of it, thirty-nine times before I was satisfied.

Interviewer: Was there some technical problem there? What was it that had stumped you?

Hemingway: Getting the words right.

Interviewer: Is it the re-reading that gets the "juice" up?

Hemingway: Re-reading places you at the point where it *has* to go on, knowing it is as good as you can get it up to there. There is always juice somewhere.

Interviewer: But are there times when the inspiration isn't there at all?

Hemingway: Naturally. But if you stopped when you knew what would happen next, you can go on. As long as you can start, you are all right. The juice will come.

Interviewer: Thornton Wilder speaks of mnemonic devices that get the writer going on his day's work. He says you once told him you sharpened twenty pencils.

Hemingway: I don't think I ever owned twenty pencils at one time. Wearing down seven No. 2 pencils is a good day's work.

Interviewer: Where are some of the places you have found most advantageous to work? The Ambos Mundos hotel must have been one, judging from the number of books you did there. Or do surroundings have little effect on the work?

Hemingway: The Ambos Mundos in Havana was a very good place to work in. This Finca is a splendid place, or was. But I have worked well everywhere. I mean I have been able to work as well as I can under varied circumstances. The telephone and visitors are the work destroyers.

Interviewer: Is emotional stability necessary to write well. You told me once that you could only write well when you were in love. Could you expound on that a bit more?

Hemingway: What a question. But full marks for trying. You can write any time people will leave you alone and not interrupt you. Or rather you can if you will be ruthless enough about it. But the best writing is certainly when you are in love. If it is all the same to you I would rather not expound on that.

Interviewer: How about financial security? Can that be a detriment to good writing?

Hemingway: If it came early enough and you loved life as much as you loved your work it would take much character to resist the temptations. Once writing has become your major vice and greatest pleasure only death can stop it. Financial security then is a great help as it keeps you from worrying. Worry destroys the ability to write. Ill health is bad in the ratio that it produces worry which attacks your subconscious and destroys your reserves.

Interviewer: Can you recall an exact moment when you decided to become a writer?

Hemingway: No, I always wanted to be a writer.

Interviewer: Philip Young in his book on you suggests that the traumatic shock of your severe 1918 mortar wound had a great influence on you as a writer. I remember in Madrid you talked briefly about his thesis, finding little in it, and going on to say that you thought the artist's equipment was not an acquired characteristic, but inherited, in the Mendelian sense.

Hemingway: Evidently in Madrid that year my mind could not be

called very sound. The only thing to recommend it would be that I
spoke only briefly about Mr. Young's book and his trauma theory of
literature. Perhaps the two concussions and a skull fracture of that
year had made me irresponsible in my statements. I do remember
telling you that I believed imagination could be the result of inherited
racial experience. It sounds all right in good jolly post-concussion
talk, but I think that is more or less where it belongs. So until the next
liberation trauma, let's leave it there. Do you agree? But thanks for
leaving out the names of any relatives I might have implicated. The
fun of talk is to explore, but much of it and all that is irresponsible
should not be written. Once written you have to stand by it. You may
have said it to see whether you believed it or not. On the question
you raised, the effects of wounds vary greatly. Simple wounds which
do not break bone are of little account. They sometimes give
confidence. Wounds which do extensive bone and nerve damage are
not good for writers, nor anybody else.

Interviewer: What would you consider the best intellectual training for the would-be writer?

Hemingway: Let's say that he should go out and hang himself
because he finds that writing well is impossibly difficult. Then he
should be cut down without mercy and forced by his own self to
write as well as he can for the rest of his life. At least he will have the
story of the hanging to commence with.

Interviewer: How about people who've gone into the academic
career? Do you think the large number of writers who hold teaching
positions have compromised their literary careers?

Hemingway: It depends on what you call compromise. Is the
usage that of a woman who has been compromised? Or is it the
compromise of the statesman? Or the compromise made with your
grocer or your tailor that you will pay a little more but will pay it later?
A writer who can both write and teach should be able to do both.
Many competent writers have proved it could be done. I could not do
it, I know, and I admire those who have been able to. I would think
though that the academic life could put a period to outside experience which might possibly limit the growth of knowledge of the
world. Knowledge, however, demands more responsibility of a writer
and makes writing more difficult. Trying to write something of
permanent value is a full-time job even though only a few hours a

day are spent on the actual writing. A writer can be compared to a well. There are as many kinds of wells as there are writers. The important thing is to have good water in the well and it is better to take a regular amount out than to pump the well dry and wait for it to re-fill. I see I am getting away from the question, but the question was not very interesting.

Interviewer: Would you suggest newspaper work for the young writer? How helpful was the training you had with the *Kansas City Star?*

Hemingway: On the *Star* you were forced to learn to write a simple, declarative sentence. This is useful to anyone. Newspaper work will not harm a young writer and could help him if he gets out of it in time. This is one of the dustiest cliches there is and I apologize for it. But when you ask someone old tired questions you are apt to receive old tired answers.

Interviewer: You once wrote in the *Transatlantic Review* that the only reason for writing journalism was to be well-paid. You said: "And when you destroy the valuable things you have by writing about them, you want to get big money for it." Do you think of writing as a type of self-destruction?

Hemingway: I do not remember ever writing that. But it sounds silly and violent enough for me to have said it to avoid having to bite on the nail and make a sensible statement. I certainly do not think of writing as a type of self-destruction though journalism, after a point has been reached, can be a daily self-destruction for a serious creative writer.

Interviewer: Do you think the intellectual stimulus of the company of other writers is of any value to an author?

Hemingway: Certainly.

Interviewer: In the Paris of the twenties did you have any sense of "group feeling" with other writers and artists?

Hemingway: No. There was no group feeling. We had respect for each other. I respected a lot of painters, some of my own age, others older—Gris, Picasso, Braque, Monet, who was still alive then—and a few writers: Joyce, Ezra, the good of Stein . . .

Interviewer: When you are writing, do you ever find yourself influenced by what you're reading at the time?

Hemingway: Not since Joyce was writing *Ulysses.* His was not a direct influence. But in those days when words we knew were barred to us, and we had to fight for a single word, the influence of his work was what changed everything, and made it possible for us to break away from the restrictions.

Interviewer: Could you learn anything about writing from the writers? You were telling me yesterday that Joyce, for example, couldn't bear to talk about writing.

Hemingway: In company with people of your own trade you ordinarily speak of other writers' books. The better the writers the less they will speak about what they have written themselves. Joyce was a very great writer and he would only explain what he was doing to jerks. Others writers that he respected were supposed to be able to know what he was doing by reading it.

Interviewer: You seem to have avoided the company of writers in late years. Why?

Hemingway: That is more complicated. The further you go in writing the more alone you are. Most of your best and oldest friends die. Others move away. You do not see them except rarely, but you write and have much the same contact with them as though you were together at the cafe in the old days. You exchange comic, sometimes cheerfully obscene and irresponsible letters, and it is almost as good as talking. But you are more alone because that is how you must work and the time to work is shorter all the time and if you waste it you feel you have committed a sin for which there is no forgiveness.

Interviewer: What about the influence of these people—your contemporaries—on your work? What was Gertrude Stein 's contribution, if any? Or Ezra Pound's? Or Max Perkins'?

Hemingway: I'm sorry but I am no good at these post-mortems. There are coroners literary and non-literary provided to deal with such matters. Miss Stein wrote at some length and with considerable inaccuracy about her influence on my work. It was necessary for her to do this after she had learned to write dialogue from a book called *The Sun Also Rises*. I was very fond of her and thought it was splendid she had learned to write conversation. It was no new thing to me to learn from everyone I could, living or dead, and I had no idea it would affect Gertrude so violently. She already wrote very well in other ways. Ezra was extremely intelligent on the subjects he really knew. Doesn't this sort of talk bore you? This backyard literary gossip while washing out the dirty clothes of thirty-five years ago is disgusting to me. It would be different if one had tried to tell the whole truth. That would have some value. Here it is simpler and better to thank Gertrude for everything I learned from her about the abstract relationship of words, say how fond I was of her, re-affirm my loyalty to Ezra as a great poet and a loyal friend, and say that I cared so much for Max Perkins that I have never been able to accept that he is dead. He never asked me to change anything I wrote except to remove certain words which were not then publishable. Blanks were left, and anyone who knew the words would know what they were. For me he was not an editor. He was a wise friend and a wonderful companion. I liked the way he wore his hat and the strange way his lips moved.

Interviewer: Who would you say are your literary forebears— those you have learned the most from?

Hemingway: Mark Twain, Flaubert, Stendhal, Bach, Turgeniev, Tolstoi, Dostoevsky, Chekhov, Andrew Marvell, John Donne, Maupassant, the good Kipling, Thoreau, Captain Marryat, Shakespeare, Mozart, Quevedo, Dante, Virgil, Tintoretto, Hieronymus Bosch, Breughel, Patinier, Goya, Giotto, Cézanne, Van Gogh, Gaughuin, San Juan de la Cruz, Gongora—it would take a day to remember everyone. Then it would sound as though I were claiming an erudition I did not possess instead of trying to remember all the people who have had an influence on my life and work. This isn't an old dull question. It is a very good but a solemn question and requires an examination of conscience. I put in painters, or started to, because I learn as much from painters about how to write as from writers. You ask how this is done? It would take another day of explaining. I should think what one learns from composers and from the study of harmony and counterpoint would be obvious.

Interviewer: Did you ever play a musical instrument?

Hemingway: I used to play cello. My mother kept me out of school a whole year to study music and counterpoint. She thought I had ability, but I was absolutely without talent. We played chamber music—someone came in to play the violin; my sister played the viola, and mother the piano. That cello—I played it worse than anyone on earth. Of course, that year I was out doing other things too.

Interviewer: Do you re-read the authors of your list. Twain, for instance?

Hemingway: You have to wait two or three years with Twain. You remember too well. I read some Shakespeare every year, *Lear* always. Cheers you up if you read that.

Interviewer: Reading, then, is a constant occupation and pleasure.

Hemingway: I'm always reading books—as many as there are. I ration myself on them so that I'll always be in supply.

Interviewer: Do you ever read manuscripts?

Hemingway: You can get into trouble doing that unless you know the author personally. Some years ago I was sued for plagiarism by a man who claimed that I'd lifted *For Whom the Bell Tolls* from an unpublished screen scenario he'd written. He'd read this scenario at some Hollywood party. I was there, he said, at least there was a fellow called "Ernie" there listening to the reading, and that was enough for him to sue for a million dollars. At the same time he sued the producers of the motion-pictures *North-West Mounted Police* and the *Cisco Kid,* claiming that these, as well, had been stolen from that same unpublished scenario. We went to court and, of course, won the case. The man turned out to be insolvent.

Interviewer: Well, could we go back to that list and take one of the painters—Hieronymus Bosch, for instance? The nightmare symbolic quality of his work seems so far removed from your own.

Hemingway: I have the nightmares and know about the ones other people have. But you do not have to write them down. Anything you can omit that you know you still have in the writing and its quality will show. When a writer omits things he does not know, they show like holes in his writing.

Interviewer: Does that mean that a close knowledge of the works of the people on your list helps fill the "well" you were speaking of a while back. Or were they consciously a help in developing the techniques of writing?

Hemingway: They were a part of learning to see, to hear, to think, to feel and not feel, and to write. The well is where your "juice" is. Nobody knows what it is made of, least of all yourself. What you know is if you have it, or you have to wait for it to come back.

Interviewer: Would you admit to there being symbolism in your novels?

Hemingway: I suppose there are symbols since critics keep finding them. If you do not mind I dislike talking abut them and being questioned about them. It is hard enough to write books and stories without being asked to explain them as well. Also it deprives the explainers of work. If five or six or more good explainers can keep going why should I interfere with them? Read anything I write for the pleasure of reading it. Whatever else you find will be the measure of what you brought to the reading.

Interviewer: Continuing with just one question on this line: One of the advisory staff editors wonders about a parallel he feels he's found in *The Sun Also Rises* between the dramatis personae of the bull ring and the characters of the novel itself. He points out that the first sentence of the book tells us Robert Cohn is a boxer; later, during the desencajonada, the bull is described as using his horns like a boxer, hooking and jabbing. And just as the bull is attracted and pacified by the presence of a steer, Robert Cohn defers to Jake who is emasculated precisely as is a steer. He sees Mike as the picador, baiting Cohn repeatedly. The editor's thesis goes on, but he wondered if it was your conscious intention to inform the novel with the tragic structure of the bullfight ritual.

Hemingway: It sounds as though the advisory staff editor was a little bit screwy. Who ever said Jake was "emasculated precisely as a steer?" Actually he had been wounded in quite a different way and his testicles were intact and not damaged. Thus he was capable of all normal feelings as a *man* but incapable of consummating them. The important distinction is that his wound was physical and not psychological and that he was not emasculated.

Interviewer: These questions which inquire into craftsmanship really are an annoyance.

Hemingway: A sensible question is neither a delight nor an annoyance. I still believe though that it is very bad for a writer to talk about how he writes. He writes to be read by the eye and no explanations nor dissertations should be necessary. You can be sure that there is much more than will be read at any first reading and having made this it is not the writer's province to explain it or run guided tours through the more difficult country of his work.

Interviewer: In connection with this, I remember you have also warned that it is dangerous for a writer to talk about a work-in-progress, that he can "talk it out" so to speak. Why should this be so? I only ask because there are so many writers—Twain, Wilde, Thurber, Steffens come to mind—who would seem to have polished their material by testing it on listeners.

Hemingway: I cannot believe Twain ever "tested out" *Huckleberry Finn* on listeners. If he did they probably had him cut out good things and put in the bad parts. Wilde was said by people who knew him to have been a better talker than a writer. Steffens talked better than he wrote. Both his writing and his talking were sometimes hard to believe, and I heard many stories change as he grew older. If Thurber can talk as well as he writes he must be one of the greatest and least boring talkers. The man I know who talks best about his own trade and has the pleasantest and most wicked tongue is Juan Belmonte, the matador.

Interviewer: Could you say how much thought-out effort went into the evolvement of your distinctive style?

Hemingway: That is a long-term tiring question and if you spent a couple of days answering it you would be so self-conscious that you could not write. I might say that what amateurs call a style is usually only the unavoidable awkwardness in first trying to make something that has not heretofore been made. Almost no new classics resemble other previous classics. At first people can only see the awkwardness. Then they are not so perceptible. When they show so very awkwardly people think these awkwardnesses are the style and many copy them. This is regrettable.

Interviewer: You once wrote me that the simple circumstances under which various pieces of fiction were written could be instructive. Could you apply this to "The Killers"—you said that you had written it, "Ten Indians" and "Today is Friday" in one day—and perhaps to your first novel *The Sun Also Rises?*

Hemingway: Let's see. *The Sun Also Rises* I started in Valencia on my birthday, July 21st. Hadley, my wife, and I had gone to Valencia early to get good tickets for the Feria there which started the 24th of July. Everybody my age had written a novel and I was still having a difficult time writing a paragraph. So I started the book on my birthday, wrote all through the Feria, in bed in the morning, went on to Madrid and wrote there. There was no Feria there, so we had a room with a table and I wrote in great luxury on the table and around the corner from the hotel in a beer place in the Pasaje Alvarez where it was cool. It finally got too hot to write and we went to Hendaye. There was a small cheap hotel there on the big long lovely beach and I worked very well there and then went up to Paris and finished the first draft in the apartment over the sawmill at 113 rue Notre-Dame-des-Champs six weeks from the day I started it. I showed the first draft to Nathan Asch, the novelist, who then had quite a strong accent and he said "Hem, vaht do you mean saying you wrote a novel? A novel huh. Hem you are riding a travhel büch." I was not too discouraged by Nathan and rewrote the book, keeping in the travel (that was the part about the fishing trip and Pamplona) at Schruns in the Vorarlberg at the Hotel Taube.

The stories you mention I wrote in one day in Madrid on May 16 when it snowed out the San Isidro bullfights. First I wrote "The Killers" which I'd tried to write before and failed. Then after lunch I got in bed to keep warm and wrote "Today is Friday." I had so much juice I thought maybe I was going crazy and I had about six other stories to write. So I got dressed and walked to Fornos, the old bull fighter's cafe, and drank coffee and then came back and wrote *Ten Indians*. This made me very sad and I drank some brandy and went to sleep. I'd forgotten to eat and one of the waiters brought me up some Bacalao and a small steak and fried potatoes and a bottle of Valdepeñas.

The woman who ran the Pension was always worried that I did not eat enough and she had sent the waiter. I remember sitting up in bed and eating, and drinking the Valdepeñas. The waiter said he would bring up another bottle. He said the Señora wanted to know if I was going to write all night. I said no, I thought I would lay off for a while. Why don't you try to write just one more, the waiter asked. I'm only supposed to write one, I said. Nonsense, he said. You could write six. I'll try tomorrow, I said. Try it tonight, he said. What do you think the old woman sent the food up for?

I'm tired, I told him. Nonsense, he said (the word was not nonsense). You tired after three miserable little stories. Translate me one.

Leave me alone, I said. How am I going to write it if you don't leave me alone. So I sat up in bed and drank the Valdepeñas and thought what a hell of a writer I was if the first story was as good as I'd hoped.

Interviewer: How complete in your own mind is the conception of a short story? Does the theme, or the plot, or a character change as you go along?

Hemingway: Sometimes you know the story. Sometimes you make it up as you go along and have no idea how it will come out. Everything changes as it moves. That is what makes the movement which makes the story. Sometimes the movement is so slow it does not seem to be moving. But there is always change and always movement.

Interviewer: Is it the same with the novel, or do you work out the whole plan before you start and adhere to it rigorously?

Hemingway: *For Whom The Bell Tolls* was a problem which I carried on each day. I knew what was going to happen in principle. But I invented what happened each day as I wrote.

Interviewer: Were the *Green Hills of Africa, To Have and Have Not,* and *Across the River and Into the Trees* all started as short stories and developed into novels? If so, are the two forms so similar that the writer can pass from one to the other without completely revamping his approach?

Hemingway: No, that is not true. The *Green Hills of Africa* is not a novel but was written in an attempt to write an absolutely true book to see whether the shape of a country and the pattern of a month's action could, if truly presented, compete with a work of the imagination. After I had written it I wrote two short stories, "The Snows of Kilimanjaro" and "The Short Happy Life of Francis Macomber." These were stories which I invented from the knowledge and experience acquired on the same long hunting trip one month of which I had tried to write a truthful account of in *The Green Hills. To Have and Have Not* and *Across the River and Into the Trees* were both started as short stories.

Interviewer: Do you find it easy to shift from one literary project to another or do you continue through to finish what you start?

Hemingway: The fact that I am interrupting serious work to answer these questions proves that I am so stupid that I should be penalized severely. I will be. Don't worry.

Interviewer: Do you think of yourself in competiton with other writers?

Hemingway: Never. I used to try to write better than certain dead writers of whose value I was certain. For a long time now I have tried simply to write the best I can. Sometimes I have good luck and write better than I can.

Interviewer: Do you think a writer's power diminishes as he grows older? In the *Green Hills of Africa* you mention that American writers at a certain age change into Old Mother Hubbards.

Hemingway: I don't know about that. People who know what they are doing should last as long as their heads last. In that book you mention, if you look it up, you'll see I was sounding off about American literature with a humorless Austrian character who was forcing me to talk when I wanted to do something else. I wrote an accurate account of the conversation. Not to make deathless pronouncements. A fair percent of the pronouncements are good enough.

Interviewer: We've not discussed character. Are the characters of your work taken without exception from real life?

Hemingway: Of course they are not. *Some* come from real life. Mostly you invent people from a knowledge and understanding and experience of people.

Interviewer: Could you say something about the process of turning a real-life character into a fictional one?

Hemingway: If I explained how that is sometimes done, it would be a handbook for libel lawyers.

Interviewer: Do you make a distinction—as E. M. Forster does—between "flat" and "round" characters?

Hemingway: If you describe someone, it is flat, as a photograph is, and from my standpoint a failure. If you make him up from what you know, there should be all the dimensions.

Interviewer: Which of your characters do you look back on with particular affection?

Hemingway: That would make too long a list.

Interviewer: Then you enjoy reading over your own books—without feeling there are changes you would like to make?

Hemingway: I read them sometimes to cheer me up when it is hard to write and then I remember that it was always difficult and how nearly impossible it was sometimes.

Interviewer: How do you name your characters?

Hemingway: The best I can.

Interviewer: Do the titles come to you while you're in the process of doing the story?

Hemingway: No. I make a list of titles *after* I've finished the story or the book—sometimes as many as 100. Then I start eliminating them, sometimes all of them.

Interviewer: And you do this even with a story whose title is supplied from the text—"Hills Like White Elephants," for example?

Hemingway: Yes. The title comes afterwards. I met a girl in Prunier where I'd gone to eat oysters before lunch. I knew she'd had an abortion. I went over and we talked, not about that, but on the way home I thought of the story, skipped lunch, and spent that afternoon writing it.

Interviewer: So when you're not writing, you remain constantly the observer, looking for something which can be of use.

Hemingway: Surely. If a writer stops observing he is finished. But he does not have to observe consciously nor think how it will be useful. Perhaps that would be true at the beginning. But later everything he sees goes into the great reserve of things he knew or has seen. If it is any use to know it, I always try to write on the principle of the iceberg. There is seven-eights of it underwater for every part that shows. Anything you know you can eliminate and it only strengthens your iceberg. It is the part that doesn't show. If a writer omits something because he does not know it then there is a hole in the story.

The Old Man and the Sea could have been over a thousand pages long and had every character in the village in it and all the processes of how they made their living, were born, educated, bore children, etc. That is done excellently and well by other writers. In writing you are limited by what has already been done satisfactorily. So I have tried to learn to do something else. First I have tried to eliminate everything unnecessary to conveying experience to the reader so that after he or she has read something it will become a part of his or her experience and seem actually to have happened. This is very hard to do and I've worked at it very hard.

Anyway, to skip how it is done, I had unbelievable luck this time and could convey the experience completely and have it be one that no one had ever conveyed. The luck was that I had a good man and a good boy and lately writers have forgotten there still are such things. Then the ocean is worth writing about just as man is. So I was lucky there. I've seen the marlin mate and know about that. So I leave that out. I've seen a school (or pod) of more than fifty sperm whales in that same stretch of water and once harpooned one nearly sixty feet in length and lost him. So I left that out. All the stories I know from the fishing village I leave out. But the knowledge is what makes the underwater part of the iceberg.

Interviewer: Archibald MacLeish has spoken of a technical device you discovered which would seem to do with conveying experience to a reader. He said you developed it while covering baseball games back in those *Kansas City Star* days. It was simply that a writer should concentrate during moments of apparent inactivity—that what he described of those moments had an *effect*, and a powerful one, of making the reader conscious of what he had been aware of only subconsciously . . .

Hemingway: The anecdote is apocryphal. I never wrote baseball for the *Star*. What Archie was trying to remember was how I was trying to learn in Chicago in around 1920 and was searching for the unnoticed things that made emotions such as the way an outfielder tossed his glove without looking back to where it fell, the squeak of resin on canvas under a fighter's flat-soled gym-shoes, the gray colour of Jack Blackburn's skin when he had just come out of stir and other things I noted as a painter sketches. You saw Blackburn's strange colour and the old razor cuts and the way he spun a man before you knew his history. These were the things which moved you before you knew the story.

Interviewer: Have you ever described any type of situation of which you had no personal knowledge?

Hemingway: That is a strange question. By personal knowledge do you mean carnal knowledge? In that case the answer is positive. A writer, if he is any good, does not describe. He invents or *makes* out of knowledge personal and impersonal and sometimes he seems to have unexplained knowledge which could come from forgotten racial or family experience. Who teaches the homing pigeon to fly as he does; where does a fighting bull get his bravery, or a hunting-dog his nose? This is an elaboration or a condensation on that stuff we were talking in Madrid that time when my head was not to be trusted.

Interviewer: How detached must you be from an experience before you can write about it in fictional terms? The African air-crashes, for instance?

Hemingway: It depends on the experience. One part of you sees it with complete detachment from the start. Another part is very involved. I think there is no rule about how soon one should write about it. It would depend on how well adjusted the individual was and on his or her recuperative powers. Certainly it is valuable to a trained writer to crash in an aircraft which burns. He learns several important things very quickly. Whether they will be of use to him is conditioned by survival. Survival, with honor, that outmoded and all-important word, is as difficult as ever and as all important to a writer. Those who do not last are always more beloved since no one has to see them in their long, dull, unrelenting, no quarter given and no quarter received, fights that they make to do something as they believe it should be done before they die. Those who die or quit early and easy and with every good reason are preferred because they are understandable and human. Failure and well-disguised cowardice are more human and more beloved.

Interviewer: Could I ask you to what extent you think the writer should concern himself with the socio-political problems of his times?

Hemingway: Everyone has his own conscience and there should be no rules about how a conscience should function. All you can be sure about in a political-minded writer is that if his work should last you will have to skip the politics when you read it. Many of the so-called politically enlisted writers change their politics frequently. This is very exciting to them and to their political-literary reviews. Sometimes they even have to rewrite their view-points . . . and in a hurry. Perhaps it can be respected as a form of the pursuit of happiness.

Interviewer: Has the political influence of Ezra Pound on the segregationalist Kasper had any effect on your belief that the poet ought to be released from St. Elizabeth's Hospital.*

Hemingway: No. None at all. I believe that Ezra should be released and allowed to write poetry in Italy on an undertaking by

*As this issue went to press a Federal Court in Washington, D.C. dismissed all charges against Pound, clearing the way for his release from St. Elizabeth's.

him to abstain from any politics. I would be happy to see Kasper jailed as soon as possible. Great poets are not necessarily girl guides nor scoutmasters nor splendid influences on youth. To name a few: Verlaine, Rimbaud, Shelley, Byron, Baudelaire, Proust, Gide should not have been confined to prevent them from being aped in their thinking, their manners or their morals by local Kaspers. I am sure that it will take a footnote to this paragraph in ten years to explain who Kasper was.*

Interviewer: Would you say, ever, that there is any didactic intention in your work?

Hemingway: Didactic is a word that has been misused and has spoiled. *Death in the Afternoon* is an instructive book.

Interviewer: It has been said that a writer only deals with one or two ideas throughout his work. Would you say your work reflects one or two ideas.

Hemingway: Who said that? It sounds much too simple. The man who said it possibly *had* only one or two ideas.

Interviewer: Well, perhaps it would be better put this way: Graham Greene said in one of these interviews that a ruling passion gives to a shelf of novels the unity of a system. You yourself have said, I believe, that great writing comes out of a sense of injustice. Do you consider it important that a novelist be dominated in this way— by some such compelling sense?

Hemingway: Mr. Greene has a facility for making statements that I do not possess. It would be impossible for me to make generalizations about a shelf of novels or a wisp of snipe or a gaggle of geese. I'll try a generalization though. A writer without a sense of justice and of injustice would be better off editing the Year Book of a school for exceptional children than writing novels. Another generalization. You see; they are not so difficult when they are sufficiently obvious. The most essential gift for a good writer is a built-in, shock-proof, shit detector. This is the writer's radar and all great writers have had it.

Interviewer: Finally, a fundamental question: namely, as a creative writer what do you think is the function of your art? Why a representation of fact, rather than fact itself.

*John Kasper, organizer of the Seaboard White Citizens Council, had been found guilty of contempt of federal court in 1956—MJB.

Hemingway: Why be puzzled by that? From things that have happened and from things as they exist and from all things that you know and all those you cannot know, you make something through your invention that is not a representation but a whole new thing truer than anything true and alive, and you make it alive, and if you make it well enough, you give it immortality. That is why you write and for no other reason that you know of. But what about all the reasons that no one knows?

Hemingway Talking

Milt Machlin/1958

Reprinted, by permission of Milt Machlin, from *Argosy* (September 1958), 34–37, 84–86.

The last time I saw Papa he nearly flattened me. Of course, it was all a misunderstanding. But still, I figured The Boss overestimated my influence with Ernest Hemingway, the Great White Father of American literature, and the greatest adventure writer that ever was.

"You claim to be such a buddy of Hemingway's," The Boss told me. "Why don't you go down to Cuba and ask him what's new?"

Before you could say "Farewell to Arms," I was hustled onto a plane, and the next thing I knew I was wrestling with a giant Daiquiri in Havana's Floridita bar. This particular Daiquiri was called a Papa's Special because it was invented by Hemingway. It contained a squirt of lime, a squirt of grapefruit juice, some ice, and four ounces of rum. It usually takes me about a pint of rum just to get up the nerve to *call* Papa at his fortress, Finca Vigia, in San Francisco de Paula, about twenty miles from Havana.

The situation was this. One: Hemingway is the world's greatest writer and authority on hunting, fishing, drinking and other manly occupations. Two: This is Hemingway's year, being the year in which no less than three new Hemingway films are on view to the public. Three: The most recent Hemingway opus is the guttiest, fishiest, *masculinest* fish story ever to reach the silver screen—*The Old Man and the Sea.*

That was the situation from The Boss's point of view. From Hemingway's point of view it was a little different.

One: Papa hates interviews and doesn't give them except when his arm is twisted, and who'd want to do *that?*

Two: Papa wouldn't give two baits in a bucket for all the movies ever filmed, including the Hemingway masterpiece.

Three: Papa is now writing the most comprehensive work of his life, rumored to be a series of anywhere from three to six novels

130

dealing largely with World War II and thereafter, and is in no mood to be interrupted. When Papa is working he doesn't answer phones. When he is not working he answers them sometimes, if he feels like it, and if the caller can explain in Spanish to René. the houseboy who answers the phone, what is on his mind. When Papa is not working, he prefers fishing, on the *Pilar,* his forty-two-foot "fishing machine," for white marlin, if they are running, or for anything else big and exciting enough, if they aren't.

Papa is a very kind man. Everybody says so and it is true. But Papa is a man to whom privacy is a precious thing. The first time I saw Papa I sloped up to his verandah uninvited while Papa was reading his mail and having his evening medication of MacNish. This was before the great African plane accident in which he jammed his spine, ruptured his right kidney, collapsed his intestine and suffered a concussion. This was when Papa was in magnificent condition. Having heard tales of journalists being forcibly bounced from the premises by the master himself, I had fortified myself in the village with a local anaesthetic—barreled rum.

I rapped on the door frame with authority. There was a pained roar from inside the comfortable Spanish-style house.

"What the hell do you want?"

I explained my pilgrimage.

"What in hell do you think I moved out here for?" Papa asked, and answered his own question: "To get away from bastards like you!"

This was where the rum-priming I'd done in village paid off. I was fearless.

"Look, Mr. Hemingway," I said with simple dignity. "I was brushed off this afternoon by your houseboy, then by your maid. I've made up my mind that I'm either going to be brushed off by the boss himself or—or something."

I guess it was my fearless reply that reached him, because he asked me to come in, sit down, have a drink, have a chat, and don't print anything. This was a big fat help, but I figured, what the hell. No point in going home thirsty.

I don't know about Papa, but I had a high old time that afternoon, drinking and talking. Papa likes to drink and he likes to talk. A fifth and a half of scotch later we had touched on the subjects of: women (Spanish, French, Italian, Japanese and Greek); fish (trout, marlin,

and *sierra en escabeche;* a type of pickled *cero* mackerel); sports-
writers (he likes Jimmy Cannon); fighters (Joe Louis); ballplayers
(DiMaggio, who else?); wine (*valpolicella, orvieto, manzanilla);* beer
(he once wrote an endorsement for an American brand), and
football, among other things.

I might say that Papa is an expert in all these things and more. But,
surprisingly, he listens more than he talks, and if you don't watch out
you're *giving* him an interview instead of *getting* one.

When we got to football, I started to explain how the outside tackle
pulled out to run interference at my alma mater, dear old Brown.
Papa was demonstrating how centers immobilized tackles when he
played for Oak Park High, in Illinois. Somehow we both ended flat
on our duffs, a condition Miss Mary, Hemingway's blonde wife,
found us in when she came to announce that it was time for Papa to
go to dinner and for me to go home. I guess she was right. I went
home, and before I went Papa promised me that *next* time he'd give
me a *real, real* interview.

Six months ago I popped in on Papa again. The revolution was in
full swing down in Cuba. I showed up in the middle of the night in a
set of GI fatigues, dark glasses and sneakers. When the excitement
died down (this was the time I nearly got flattened), it was explained
that there were things you didn't do around Finca Vigia. You didn't
come unannounced, especially in the middle of the night during a
revolution. You didn't do this, especially if you were wearing noiseless
sneakers. You didn't wear fatigues or Army clothes anywhere in Cuba
unless you were ready to shoot it out with one side or the other. And
you didn't come without an invitation more recent than five years
old. Still, Papa was gracious.

We did some drinking and we talked about Paris (Dome, Coupole,
and the changes since the war); fighters (he still liked Louis but
admired Ray Robinson, too), magazines (he got some of his first
rejection slips from *Argosy*), and why I couldn't have the story I
wanted. I, at that time, was interested in Hemingway's gun collection.

"In the first place, I don't collect guns. I have some guns I like to
shoot with. I like my Springfield 30-06. But it isn't a good idea to
keep guns around the house in times like these."

It wasn't even a good idea to talk about them much, I gathered.

Papa didn't look so good. He'd put on some weight and was

drinking only a little light wine. He had something of a gut. Papa generally goes to bed about ten at night since the accident. Part of his kindness is that he doesn't seem to have the nerve to put out a guest once a pleasant drinking-talking relationship has been established. But Miss Mary serves well as watchdog and conscience. At nine-thirty she cleared her throat, and at nine-thirty-five I was shaking hands, headed for the door, with a promise that *next* time, "true," I'd get a real story.

On my third go-round with Papa I discovered certain things. Papa will never break a promise to a friend, or even an acquaintance, but Papa is not going to louse up his work schedule for anyone. From just after daylight to at least one-thirty in the afternoon, Hemingway writes in a white tower (really) which surmounts the Finca Vigia and is probably responsible for its name (it means "Lookout Ranch" and commands a startling view of Havana and the surrounding countryside).

After three days of trying, I reached Papa on the phone. He said he'd be glad to see me sometime but was not free at the moment to talk. He'd call me when he was ready.

After another day or so I had lost $150 playing a nervous game of blackjack in the casino of the Hotel Riviera, where I was staying, waiting impatiently for the phone to ring.

Time passed. I cast about for the bait that would hook Papa before I ran out of expense money and was left to work my way back on a banana boat. I looked up all of Papa's old friends. I went to Cojimar, the fishing village where he docks his boat, and talked to the fishermen who knew him. I talked to his boatman, Gregorio Fuentes, a Canary Islander, who is celebrating his twentieth year of skippering the *Pilar.* I talked to Elicio Arguelles, millionaire Cuban sportsman who is Papa's principal fishing buddy, along with Arguelles' cousin, Mayito Menocal, another millionaire Cuban sportsman. I found out that Papa's friends are almost all Cubans, and none, as far as I could determine, are writers or in any other way connected with the arts. Aside from being a writer and a great reader, Papa is one of the most unartistic bastards you'd ever meet, to the external eye.

Finally, almost by accident, I hit it. I was reading Papa a tidbit, on the phone, about *Old Man and the Sea,* from a Warner Brothers handout I happened to have with me. The item referred to Arguelles

in an ambiguous way, which I called to Papa's attention. I indicated
that I had other releases put out by the movie people and—who
knows?—maybe they were confusing too, if not downright inaccurate. Papa hit the bait like a myopic marlin.

"Be out here at six-thirty and bring those Warner things with you!"
he growled.

At six-twenty-five, Cuban photographer Tony Ortega and I rolled
up to Papa's white-painted gate. There was a big sign: NO VISITORS
EXCEPT BY APPOINTMENT. For the first time I had one.

I noticed a new adornment on Papa's front gate since my last visit.
About five rows of sharp barbed wire topped the fence around
Hemingway's fifteen-acre property and entrance gate. I asked the old
man who watched Papa's gate for him what was the pitch. Rebels?

"*Ladrones de mangos.*" He grinned through his toothless gums.

Mango thieves? That's all I could get out of the old man. It was
already dark. We drove up the unlighted road serenaded by the
cackle of chickens, barking of dogs, grunting of pigs, and crying of
children, which welled up from the houses joining Papa's property on
our right. Over this came the throb of a *danson* from the overloud
juke box of the town bar a quarter of a mile away.

Papa greeted us at the door. He was friendly, but restrained. For
one thing, the photographer made him nervous. I promised we
wouldn't take any photos, but Tony begged for one shot for his own
use.

Papa said, "I'd rather take a punch in the nose," but he posed.

I've never seen a man so scared by a camera. He froze.

"You guys are always trying to make a guy look foolish. What are
you trying to do?" he asked Tony. "Get me with my mouth open?
This is Sunday. I'm trying to take it easy. I'm no movie star. Put away
the camera."

He was terrified. I'd discovered the one thing Papa was afraid of! I
told Tony to pack away his Rollei.

"Look," said Papa, "it's Sunday. I don't get much time to relax. If
you want to talk and take it easy, okay. Otherwise. . . " He dismissed
the subject. "Want a drink?"

I accepted a scotch. He handed me the bottle to pour for myself,
and eyed me critically as I poured.

"Lost some weight, didn't you?"

I had noticed before that he had a phenomenal memory, even recalling most of the details of that first meeting five years earlier. He stood up. He was wearing a sleeveless Cuban *guayaberra*—a sort of pleated sports shirt which hangs outside the trousers, and English-style shorts which he wears habitually around the house and the boat. The pants were about six inches too big around the waist. He unbuckled his belt and patted the flat place where his gut was the last time I had seen him.

"I lost, too. I'm down to two hundred and seven. That's a good weight for me."

He looked at me again. Even minus thirty pounds, I'm no lightweight.

"Get any exercise?" he asked.

I acknowledged that I ran for the subway with some regularity, but that was all.

"No good. You should get exercise regularly. You got to start to watch out for heart attacks and things." He patted his stomach again. "I do the eight-eighty down in the pool every day."

Sitting down, he leafed through the Warner releases I had brought, reading intensely and quickly as I looked around the forty-foot living room.

On the walls were an assortment of trophies, including a huge cape buffalo and many graceful deer and antelope. There were also bullfight posters and, on one wall, a jai-alai cesta. On the floor was a wall-to-wall Tahitian grass mat. The room was furnished comfortably with old-fashioned stuffed armchairs and some Cuban wicker and mahogany chairs. Between two armchairs stood the bar, with an assortment of spirits and some wine.

Hemingway snorted over a release claiming he had presented a cup to Batista.

"That's a lot of crap. I never saw the man!" Otherwise, he seemed satisfied. He wasn't inclined to talk about *The Old Man and the Sea,* though.

"Kid, I don't want to talk about the picture until I talk with Hayward (Leland Hayward, the producer). It's like a magician who's trying to saw a woman in half. He doesn't tell the audience how it's done before he does it, does he?"

I saw there was something that bothered him about the picture, but he wasn't inclined to tell me what it was. He did say that he pretty much liked it and that it was true to the book. According to published reports, he got $250,000 for the rights to the Nobel-prize-winning novelette, plus a one-third share of the profits, splitting equally with Hayward and the picture's star, Spencer Tracy. This is the most he ever got for film rights, and this is the only picture in which he has accepted participation.

Somehow Hemingway has always got the dirty end of the stick on movie deals. For *To Have and Have Not,* now being made, against his protest, for the third time, he got a measly $10,000. For *The Sun Also Rises,* he got nothing, having granted the rights to his first wife, who sold them for $10,000. *The Killers,* the picture he has despised least of those made from his works, earned him $37,500 and contained less than five minutes of his own dialogue.

The Old Man and the Sea retains the Hemingway dialogue almost intact, in the form of a running comment behind the action of the world's most classic fish story. It's a tale of the three-day battle between Santiago, an old Cuban drift-fisherman, and the biggest marlin ever seen, and how, after capturing the fish, the old man must fight futilely to the last ounce of his strength against the sharks which eventually claim his catch.

The setting is the little fishing village of Cojimar, a few miles from Hemingway's home. Papa knows almost every fisherman in this town personally and by name. He prides himself on his acquaintanceships with professionals, who are the only ones he really enjoys swapping fish talk with.

When *The Old Man and the Sea* came out, there was a rash of guesses as to who the "real" old man was. Some said it was an old fisherman named Anselmo who lived in Cojimar. Another old water-front habitué told journalists that *he* was the old man.

Hemingway fumed. He dragged the old pretender into the Teraza, Cojimar's famous sea-food restaurant, and had him face a kangaroo court of his fellow townspeople. The pretender confessed not only that he wasn't the old man, but that he wasn't even a fisherman.

"Then why did you say you were the old man?" Hemingway asked.

"Because they gave me five dollars."

Papa says all this speculation as to the identity of the old man is bushwah.

"The story is fiction—the conflict between a man and a fish. The old man is nobody in particular. That's stupid. A lot of people have been claiming that this person is the old man and somebody else is the kid. That's a lot of bull. I wrote that story from thirty years of fishing around here, and before that, too. Most of these fishermen in Cojimar have had experiences like that. One was out two days with a fish, and when they found him he was out of his mind. That's even worse than what my old man experienced.

"If the old man is anybody, it's Chago's father, who died four years ago. I fished with him many times."

"Chago" is Santiago Puig, the elder, a fisherman Hemingway met in his early days in Cuba. His son, who has the same name and also became a friend of Hemingway's, follows the same occupation and acted as a stand-in and occasional double for Spencer Tracy. We met him later and he told us this story of the meeting between Hemingway and his father, the man who, Papa said, is "as much the real old man as anybody."

"We were fishing in my father's boat, the small boat you see in the movie which they bought from me for fourteen hundred dollars, and took to Hollywood. We had caught a big marlin and we were having trouble boating it. I was still a young boy then (he's in his late forties now). Hemingway came along in his boat and helped us. Afterward, he asked if we wanted a drink. My father said he would like a drink of water, but Papa gave him a beer. Papa asked if he could have the head and sword of the marlin for the honor of it, and my father was proud to give it to him. Then he tried to give my father five dollars for it, but my father said he would throw the money in the sea if Papa did not take it back. So Papa took it back but said they would be friends, and they fished together many times after that"

The villain of the picture is the shark, naturally. In real life, Hemingway has been an implacable enemy of the shark. "I think it is the one thing he really hates," a friend said of him.

The first big fish Papa ever hooked, a tuna he battled for hours off Key West, was finally gotten by a shark. That night Papa turned up with a submachine gun which he persuaded millionaire Bill Leeds to give or sell him. Since then, he's gone after shark with tommyguns, rifles, shotguns and a .22.

"With the .22, it's a brain shot," says Hemingway. "You have to know the spot and hit them just right when they surface." He hits them, too.

Papa has an invention all his own for sharks. It's a wooden lance about twelve feet long, with a blade honed from a Ford spring leaf, and tempered. He always has two or three of these aboard the *Pilar.*

It's part of sport-fishing history, of course, that he brought in the first tuna in the Bahamas undamaged by shark.

"Hell," he says, "I brought in the first *two*. You got to boat them fast to keep the sharks off. If you let them get tired or sluggish, that's when the sharks move in."

His pal Arguelles says Papa boated that first tuna in two hours.

"He was fishing barefoot, and by the time he was finished, the bottoms of his feet were cut and bloody from holding against the fighting chair." It was largely by dint of sheer physical strength that Papa was able to pull those fish in—with a stiff, unyielding rod, at that.

Underneath Papa's hatred, though, is a deep respect for some sharks. The mako—*dentuso* in Spanish—is the first shark to strike the old man's marlin in Hemingway's story.

"He's not a carrion eater," says Papa. "He chases and overtakes the fastest game fish in the sea. He'll fight as good as any sport fish, too, when you hook him." Talking, Papa almost verged into admiration for this champion of sharks. This was something he liked to talk about.

"Hammerheads and tigers will attack if they're hungry or if the water is roily. Some of them are dangerous because they're dumb. A tiger will even swallow an oil can if it's hungry. Thinks it's a tortoise. Mako is a good fish—hell of a lot of action. It'll jump higher than a marlin. It's a big sport fish down in New Zealand. If you go out with the boys from Cojimar, watch out when they boat him. He smashes up a lot of good equipment. A lot of times, after they club him and harpoon him, he'll come back to life in the bottom of the boat and take a big piece out of someone's leg."

Hemingway's opinions on sharks and other fish are highly expert and respected even by museum ichthyologists. One of them once named a rosefish after him.

"There's only two sharks that are really bad. The *dentuso,* and the big white shark.

Some of these guys get near a nurse shark and when they don't get any action they say that sharks aren't dangerous. In all these movies, it's nurse sharks you see them wrestling. They wouldn't dare try that with a mako. That's why they had so much trouble trying to get shark footage for *The Old Man.* I told them to go to Bimini during the tuna run. That's when the mako are running, too. But they horsed around until it was too late, and then they went to Nassau, where there aren't any."

I could see a piece of Papa's profits bitten off like a chunk of red tuna meat. He began to think about another thing. One of the most expensive boondoggles in the making of the movie—which came in at more than double its original expected cost of $2,000,000—was the $100,000 trip Hayward sent him on to Cabo Blanco, Peru, for the big marlin.

"First we had some great footage shot in the beginning when they started making the film, but it had to be junked because it was in Cinemascope and they decided not to make the film in Cinemascope.

"Then we had this stuff shot by Fred Glasell. It was terrific, and it was of the biggest marlin ever caught—a world's record. I told Hayward we wouldn't be able to get anything better than that, but he told us to try, anyway. The biggest marlin ever caught was fourteen and a-half feet and about fifteen hundred pounds, but Hollywood wanted one eighteen feet."

Hemingway went down to Peru with Gregorio, his boat and Arguelles. Miss Mary went along, too.

"We fished for twenty-three days without getting a bite. The fun was out of it anyway, because we had to use such heavy lines to simulate the hand line in the picture, that even if we caught one it wouldn't be anything. Arguelles boated a nine-hundred-pounder in two hours on the heavy line. We finally got three or four big ones and sent them back to Havana, but they weren't big enough, and they didn't jump—not once. There were three boats on the job and it was costing a fortune. I offered to stay down with one boat and one camera, but by that time they had decided to give up making the picture for a while. They finally wound up using the Glasell footage anyway."

Gregorio was humiliated. He was sure that he could come up with a record breaker if they gave him enough time.

I poured myself another scotch and held out the bottle to Papa. He waved it away.

"I'll be drinking this one long after you're gone." He clutched the scotch and lime he was nursing. "I only get two a night and I have to make them last."

I told him that I'd been drinking "Papa's Specials" with a friend of his the previous night. We'd been matching capacities.

Papa looked interested and a little wistful for the old days.

"Did you break my record?"

"What was that?"

"Fifteen."

"Fifteen!" I'd gotten pretty crocked on four. "What was your time?"

"Well, from about ten-thirty in the morning, until seven o'clock at night. Guillermo (a famous jai-alai player) came into the Floridita. He was down. He'd just lost a *partido* (jai-alai game) thirty to sixteen. I said, 'Cheer up, kid, let's have a drink.' We started drinking easy, that way. It wasn't a contest, but we were still there by seven, and I went home and worked.

"I know I drank fifteen because I signed for it on the tab."

"You *worked?*"

"Wait a minute. No, I didn't work. I read." He started to figure. "How much booze was that? Let's see . . . there's four ounces in a Special . . ."

I had already figured it. "Sixty ounces—more than two fifths!"

"Of course, we drank standing up. You can drink more that way. I guess we had some *saladitos* (hors-d'oeuvres), too, and something else to eat. You have to eat something."

"What about Vasco Da Gama, down there, does that bother you?" I was referring to the bronze bust of Hemingway they have in Papa's corner of the Floridita.

"It's getting so I hardly like to go in any more. These bastards won't let you drink in peace. I don't have any privacy any more. A lot of people think the statue is of Constante (the owner). Mrs. Constante had it done down the road here."

He sipped his lime and scotch sparingly. In the old days he used to navigate his boat by the bottle. Two Fundadors north by one Bacardi east.

I asked him how he'd like to go to Russia as a correspondent for *Argosy*.

"They already asked me to go about three times—as an exchange writer, whatever that is. The State Department asked me, too. What the hell would I do? Pose for pictures, sign autographs and make a lot of speeches? I don't know the language. You can't find out a damned thing if you don't know the language. I'm okay any place they speak French, Italian, Spanish or Swahili. That's all."

Miss Mary came into the room, wearing neat white shorts with a small printed pattern, emphasizing her well-tanned legs.

"I saw you in the movies," I told her, referring to the flash of a moment she appears at the end of *The Old Man and the Sea*.

"Oh that was a silly business," she said, distracted. She turned to Papa. "Miss Puss is missing. I haven't seen her in hours."

Hemingway seemed to tense up, but he reassured Miss Mary. "Don't worry, she'll turn up."

Miss Mary retreated to the back of the house again, but after she was gone Papa seemed nervous. He stood up and listened for noises in the night. All you could hear was the insistent throbbing of drums.

I thought to myself, "The natives are restless," but realized it was only the distant boom of the juke box in San Francisco de Paula.

I asked about the recent addition of the barbed wire to the fence, and Papa looked at me sharply.

"Mango thieves?" I asked innocently.

He nodded distractedly, still listening into the night. "Maybe."

There was a sound in the darkness like a baby crying. Papa smiled and untensed.

"She's back. Miss Puss is back," he said. I realized it had been a missing cat that had upset him. There are cats all over the place at

Finca Vigía. "Just Cuban alley cats, but we love 'em," says Miss Mary.

Miss Mary came back into the room and looked at me significantly. I got the signal.

"Let me know if you want to do a story on the broadbill and sharks. That's a good story and it hasn't been done," Papa said.

I said I would, and drifted out into the drum-throbbing darkness.

Hemingway Talks to American Youth

A. E. Hotchner/1959

Reprinted from the *New York Herald Tribune* (18 October 1959), "This Week" section, 10–11, 24–26. © I. H. T. Corporation. Reprinted by permission.

Last winter, for the first time in a decade, Ernest Hemingway came back to live for a while in the United States. His home is in Cuba, and when he is not there he lives in Spain or in France, but a year ago he rented a log house in the tiny Idaho town of Ketchum, one mile from Sun Valley.

There he hunted game birds with old friends and worked hard on a new novel. One day he found a wounded owl. He kept it in the garage attached to his house, ministered to it lovingly. As the winter months passed to spring, the owl grew big and strong—and so did the new novel.

One evening, after Ernest and I had spent the day tramping through the snow fields in successful quest of our limit of wild ducks, we drove to the neighboring town of Hailey. Ernest had promised Father O'Connor, the priest of the local parish, that he would meet with the church's young people's group.

We met in the living room of the parish house where 30 or so high school teen-agers had assembled. For over an hour, Hemingway answered questions that reflected not only the literary interests of a group of today's teen-agers but also their attitudes toward the future. Listening to this exchange one couldn't help but be impressed by both the sincerity of the questions and the wisdom of the answers.

Q: Mr. Hemingway, how did you get started writing books?
A: I always wanted to write. I worked on the school paper, and my

143

first jobs were writing. After I finished high school I went to Kansas
City and worked on the *Star.* It was regular newspaper work: Who
shot who? Who broke into where? Where? When? How? But never
Why. Not really Why.

Q: About that book, *For Whom the Bell Tolls*—I know that you were
in Spain, but what were you doing there?

A: I had gone over to cover the Spanish Civil War for the North
American Newspaper Alliance. I took some ambulances over for the
Republican side.

Q: Why the Republican side?

A: I had seen the Republic start. I was there when King Alfonso left
and I watched the people write their constitution. That was the last
Republic that had started in Europe and I believed in it. I believe the
Republican side could have won the war and there would have been
an okay Republic in Spain today. Everybody mixed into that war. But
knowing Spaniards I believe the Republic would have gotten rid of all
non-Spaniards when the war was over. They don't want any other
people trying to run them.

Q: How much formal education did you have?

A: I finished Oak Park High School—that's in Illinois. I went to war
instead of college. When I came back from the war it was too late to
go to college. In those days there was no GI Bill.

Q: When you start a book, like *The Old Man and The Sea,* how do
you get the idea?

A: I knew about a man in that situation with a fish. I knew what
happened in a boat, in a sea, fighting a fish. So I took a man I knew
for 20 years and imagined him under those circumstances.

Q: How did you develop your style of writing—did you do it to be
commercial, to create a public demand?

A: In stating as fully as I could how things really were, it was often
very difficult and I wrote awkwardly and the awkwardness is what
they called my style. All mistakes and awkwardnesses are easy to see,
and they called it style.

Q: I want to ask you about your magnificent beard. I've been
thinking of growing one. What inspired your beard?

A: When you have a slight case of skin cancer from the rays of the
sun off the sea, you grow a beard and quit shaving.

Q: How long does it take you to write a book?
A: That depends on the book, and how it goes. A good book takes maybe a year and a half.
Q: How many hours a day do you work?
A: I get up at six and try not to work past 12.
Q: Twelve midnight?
A: Twelve noon.
Q: Have you ever had a failure?
A: You fail every day if you're not going good. When you first start writing you never fail. You think it's wonderful and you have a fine time. You think it's easy to write and you enjoy it very much, but you are thinking of yourself, not the reader. He does not enjoy it very much. Later, when you have learned to write for the reader, it is no longer easy to write. In fact, what you ultimately remember about anything you've written, is how difficult it was to write it.
Q: When you were young and first writing, were you frightened of criticism?
A: There is nothing to be afraid of. In the beginning I was not making any money at it and I just wrote as well as I could. I believed in what I wrote—if they didn't like it, it was their fault; they would learn to like it later. But I was really not concerned with criticism, and not in close touch with it. When you first start writing you are not noticed—that is the blessing of starting.
Q: Do you ever anticipate failure?
A: If you anticipate failure you'll have it. Of course, you are aware of what will happen if you fail, and you plan your escape routes—you would be unintelligent if you didn't—but you don't anticipate failure in the thing you do.
Q: (Father O'Connor) So many of our children fail to take any initiative—they are fearful, look only to material things—these young people are so fearful. . .
A: Now I don't want you to think I've never been spooked, but if you don't take command of your fears, no attack will ever go.
Q: Were you ever threatened about something you were writing or planning to write?
A: Well, they often said they'd like to kill me after I wrote it.
Q: Do you outline a book before you write it, or make a lot of notes?

A: No, I just start it. Fiction is inventing out of what knowledge you have. If you invent successfully, it is more true than if you try to remember it. A big lie is more plausible than truth. People who write fiction, if they had not taken it up, might have become very successful liars.

Q: (Father O'Connor) This group of boys and girls—based on your knowledge of children in other countries—are they better qualified to face society as adults?

A: As far as being qualified, it depends on what you have to face. Certainly school work is much more difficult in Europe. My sons went to school abroad, and I know children have to work much harder in schools in France and Germany than in the States. And in Russia, I understand the school burden is terrible. But I haven't gone to school for a long time.

As for facing the future as adults, if you follow something far enough your possibilities are unlimited. You settle for less, you get less. The big thing is not to settle too easy.

Q: How many books have you written?

A: I think 13. That's not very many, but I take a long time to write a book and I like to have fun in between. Also there have been too many wars and I was out of the writing business a long time.

Q: That book, A Farewell To Arms, how many years or months did it take you to write it?

A: I started it in Paris in the winter and wrote on it in Cuba, and Key West, Fla., in the early spring, then in Piggott, Ark., where my wife's parents were; then came up to Kansas City where one of my sons was born, and finished it in Big Horn, Wyo., in the fall. The first draft took eight months, and after five months to rewrite, 13 months in all.

Q: Do you ever get discouraged—did you ever quit on a book?

A: Been discouraged but can't quit—there's no place to go. You can run but you can't hide.

Q: (Father) These young people in school, they just follow the curriculum; they don't try to supplement anything on their own, could you give them some advice about that?

A: Well, I could give you a good pep talk but the truth is I played football in high school, and went right into basketball and then the track season and then baseball, and from all these sports I was always too tired to study. I learned more after I got out of school. One year I had to have a private tutor for Latin and my father made me pay for him out of dough I had to earn. I had to have this tutor because in Latin class I had been sitting next to a very bright guy who moved away, and suddenly my average slumped. There are high schools like that where football practice uses up all the study time and leaves you so tired you can't study anyway. You should be guaranteed a good guy sitting next to you in Latin.

Q: Do you think it's useful to take Latin?

A: I never regretted it. It's a good foundation for all the Romance languages; it made French, Italian and Spanish easier for me.

Q: Do you ever get your characters in a spot from which they can't escape?

A: Well, you try to avoid that or else you'll put yourself out of business.

Q: All these stories you write about Africa—why do you like Africa so much?

A: Some countries you love, some you can't stand. I love that one. There are some places here in Idaho that are like Africa and Spain. That's why so many Basques came here.

Q: Do you read a good deal?

A: Yes, all the time. After I quit writing for the day, I don't want to keep thinking about it so I read.

Q: Do you study actual people for your books?

A: I don't go where I go for that purpose; I just go where my life takes me. There are things you do because you like to do them, other things because you have to do them. In doing these things you find the people you write about.

Q: Do you enjoy pictures based on your books?

A: I usually can't stand them. The only one of those movies made by Hollywood I liked was *The Killers*. I had to walk out on all the others except *The Old Man And The Sea*. I was responsible for that one.

Q: What got you started writing *A Farewell To Arms?*

A: I was a kid who went to Italy and got involved in the war there.

Q: Do you go to the movies?

A: Yes, I see quite a lot of them. This past year, the best ones were *The Bridge On the River Kwai* and *Around the World in Eighty Days*.

Around the World starts dull and slow, but it develops a wonderful quality like a dream—that dream quality is a unique thing that a good movie can generate.

Q: Did you see *A Farewell To Arms?*

A: This last one?

Q: Yes, the one with Rock Hudson.

A: No! But I understand they loused it up.

Q: Do they ask your permission to do a movie like that?

A: For that movie they neither asked me nor paid me.

Q: When you crashed that time in Africa, was it as harrowing as you wrote about it?

A: Well, we crashed once in moderate jungle, and again when the rescue plane tried to take off.

Q: When you were down in the jungle, did you really exist on what they said you did?

A: You mean bananas and gin? We did all right. I never knew they wrote a song about that until I heard it up in Ketchum a few days ago.

Q: How did you learn so many languages?

A: By living in those countries. The Latin I had in school made language-learning easier, especially Italian. I was in Italy for quite a while during the first World War, and I picked up the language quickly and thought I spoke it rather well. But after I'd been a wounded, I had to spend some time on therapy machines, exercising my wounded leg, and I became friends with an Italian major who was also getting therapy on the machines. I told him I thought Italian was an easy language. He complimented me on how well I spoke. I said I hardly deserved compliments since it was so easy.

"In that case," he said, "you might take up some grammar." So I began to study Italian grammar and I stopped talking for several months. I found that learning all the Romance languages was made easier by reading the newspapers—an English-language paper in the morning, and then the foreign-language paper in the afternoon—it was the same news and the familiarity with the news events helped me understand the afternoon papers.

Q: After you finish a book, do you re-read it?

A: Yes. Today I re-read and re-wrote four chapters. You put down the words in hot blood, like an argument, and correct them when your temper has cooled.

Q: How long do you usually write?

A: No more than six hours. After that you're too pooped and the quality goes. When I'm working on a book I try to write every day except Sunday. I don't work on Sunday. It's very bad luck to work on a Sunday. Sometimes I do it but it's bad luck just the same.

A Visit to Havana

Kenneth Tynan/1960

Reprinted from *Holiday,* 27 (February 1960), 54, 56. Reprinted
with permission of *Travel-Holiday,* Travel Building, Floral Park,
New York.

Ernest Hemingway, who lives on a small estate in the suburb of San
Francisco de Paula, is by any standards the best-known foreigner in
Havana, where he has made his home since the Spanish Civil War.
Iron gates and a sign that reads: "No Admission Except By Appointment" deter the casual visitor. The house, hidden from the road by
trees, is low and rambling; it might belong to a retired district
commissioner who had inherited a library. Books are everywhere,
stacked on the floor, piled on the desks, tumbling off the shelves, and
trophies hang on every wall, among them the skin of a lion shot by
Miss Mary, Hemingway's wife. His workroom contains, apart from
books, wild life and unopened mail, a brass bedstead and a high,
narrow desk on which he writes in longhand, standing up. He works
every morning until lunchtime, when he pads down to the pool, dives
in and swims his daily half mile.

At home he mostly goes barefoot, wearing khaki shorts and a T
shirt. In manner and appearance he suggests an enormous boy, a
giant child made gruff by shyness. The heavyweight muscles of his
shoulders give him a stooping look, and when walking at speed he
leads with them, as if breasting a flood.

His head is a fairly heroic affair, the more so since he took to
combing his hair forward, so that it falls onto his forehead in white,
prophetic curls. A beard decorates his chin like shaving cream. His
nose, pink and shining from the sun, is sternly Roman.

So far, everything is antique splendor, and it is hard to remember
that he is sixty, and not six hundred, years old; hard, until you look at
the eyes and the mouth, which are those of a studious adolescent.
His lips are thin and sensitive, out of keeping with his massive
physique; and his eyes, pale blue behind steel-rimmed, amber-tinted

spectacles, are curiously innocent. In moments of anger they grow moist and baleful, but in fits of enthusiasm they gleam with a delighted eagerness, the lips part in a sharklike grin, and the whole heavy head nods with pleasure.

He talks in a whispering baritone with careful finality, and what he utters are judgments, not opinions; his gaze shifts warily, searching for eavesdroppers even if the room is empty, as he confides to your ear alone the *ex cathedra* truth.

Hemingway has the humility that comes of absolute certainty. When he is surrounded by a circle of sycophants, certainty tends to override humility, and he can be brutally curt with anyone who contradicts him. In smaller groups, his courtesy and gentleness are overwhelming; there is no aggressiveness, no exhibitionism, in his demeanor. A maxim occurs to me: only true egotists are spared the necessity of behaving egotistically.

Lunch *chez* Hemingway, Miss Mary presides, brisk and crisp, with tight pale skin and short blond hair, while cats parade the table. The Hemingway cat collection numbers about two dozen; Poppa points out the current chieftain, whose name is Cristobal—"a good fighting cat." We eat *cebiche,* a reviving bowl of pickled sea food, followed by broiled bluefish, fruit and coffee. Poppa offers some judgments. Scott Fitzgerald "was soft, he dissolved at the least touch of alcohol"; Hemingway has no patience with writers who can operate only in what he calls "saucedom." Of a celebrated modern novelist; "His trouble is he can't *rematur"*—a Spanish taurine verb meaning to finish a sequence of passes with the bull—"he'll give you eighty-nine *naturales* but he doesn't know how to end the series." Of death: "It's too bad there's no way of exchanging some of the dead for some of the living." He shows me a German poster paying tribute to his sixtieth birthday in 1958—twelve months too soon, for he was born in 1899. He keeps it, none the less, pinned to his wall, "because whenever I look at it I figure I've got a year on the sons of bitches." Of a Catholic writer: "He was going pretty good there for a while, but now he's a whore with a crucifix over his bed." We talk of Cojimar, the village just east of Havana that is the setting of *The Old Man and the Sea,* and Hemingway offers to take me fishing if the offshore current is right.

The current was wrong, and we did not fish, but we did venture

into the heart of Havana. Hemingway had been away from Cuba for
six months, and as soon as we reached the Floridita restaurant, his
public headquarters, there were waiters to be embraced, big-game
fishermen to be congratulated, portrait painters to be thanked,
autographs to be signed. He drinks as he writes, standing up; and his
corner of the bar contains a bronze bust that outrageously dramatizes
him, chin up and ready for martyrdom. "We cover it," he says,
"during Lent." (The use of "we" is characteristic. Whenever possible,
Hemingway avoids the first person singular, preferring to talk as if he
had a posse with him. Which, of course, he frequently has.) He
orders the double, frozen daiquiri that local usage calls a "Poppado-
ble." Meanwhile a trio of Negro singers—two guitarists and a frantic
shaker of *maracas*—welcome him with the song they composed for
him. It is called *Soy Como Soy*—"I am as I am"—and it deals with an
apologetic Lesbian who cannot, no matter how hard she tries, be as
Poppa would desire her. The trio continues with a boisterous Mau-
Mau chant that Hemingway taught them, and a moving lament for
the death of Antonio Maceo; the lyrics of the latter, which indict in
Spanish the cowardice of those who were hiding under their beds
when Maceo was ambushed and slain, were written by Hemingway
himself. He hugs the singer and, turning to me, says with a good deal
of pride, "I'm an honorary Negro." Hours afterward having dined
elsewhere, we return to the Floridita. Entering the men's room, I find
Ernest genially sparring with the Negro attendant. "When you gonna
grow old, Poppa?" says the man, chuckling as he blocks a left jab,
"when you gonna grow old?"

Two days later, in the same restaurant, there took place a tentative,
uncertain encounter, in which I introduced Hemingway to Tennessee
Williams. The two extremes of American literature—the extrovert and
the introvert, the man of action and the man of feeling—sought in
vain to make contact. Mr. Williams arrived in a yachting jacket, as if
to convince Hemingway that although he might be decadent, he was
decadent in an open-air way. He began by expressing his love of
bullfighting and his affection for a matador he had met in Spain, a
delightful fellow extremely accessible, named Antonio Ordoñez.
Ordoñez happens to be one of the people Hemingway knows best
and admires most. "Would we like him?" asked Poppa, blandly and

mischievously, and Mr. Williams replied that he thought we would. He went on to turn the talk to Hemingway's second wife, whom he knew long ago in Key West, and to inquire about the circumstances of her death. Hemingway closed this subject quite deliberately, with a parody-Hemingway sentence. "She died like everybody else," he said, leaning solemnly toward Mr. Williams, "and after that she was dead." Mr. Williams then spoke about William Faulkner, whose distraught eyes, he said, had once moved him to tears, but I cannot say that Hemingway was notably affected. As a summit conference, it achieved little beyond surface politeness, and an admission on both sides that the relative resilience of the liver and the kidneys was of supreme importance to writers everywhere. "What I admire about Hemingway," said Mr. Williams in parting, "is that he cares about honor among men and there is no quest more desperate than that." Months later I quizzed Hemingway on the subject of honor. "People who have it," he said, "never talk about it. They know it, and they confer immortality on each other." I don't know exactly what that means, but the cadence is great.

Life in the Afternoon
Robert Emmett Ginna/1962

Reprinted from *Esquire,* 57 (February 1962), 104–106, 136. Copyright © 1962 by Esquire Associates. Reprinted by permission.

In May 1958, I arrived in Havana, bent on talking with Ernest Hemingway and hopeful of persuading him to appear on television as the subject of an interview. (I was then the producer of a series called, rather loftily, *Wisdom,* in which eminent men and women of great accomplishment and seminal influence were interviewed at home about their life and work.) Hemingway had long been sought, but although there had been correspondence over a period of time, he had shied away. Accordingly, one day I had packed, as a sample, the film of an interview already made with Igor Stravinsky and a magnum of Château Latour, 1937—a claret and vintage of magnificence—and boarded a flight for Cuba.

On a sultry Cuban afternoon I was driven out to San Francisco de Paula, a village not many miles from Havana. The gates to Hemingway's home—Finca Vigia—were locked, and I handed my driver Luis some money and told him to scout around and get them opened; some local would have a key to let in tradespeople. In a few minutes we drove in and around the circular drive to the low, white house, deep in green foliage, a modest looking but commodious Spanish colonial farmhouse.

Although I had called from the Ambos Mundos the day before, Mrs. Hemingway had been evasive. She said that Hemingway was working terribly hard and should not see any callers. She promised, however, to call me after I explained that I had only wanted to

present him the Stravinsky film. But she hadn't, and I was determined to deliver it, together with the wine and a personal note saying
that the bottle was purely a gift from me to him with thanks.

I peered through the screen door and, hearing nothing nor seeing
anyone within the heavily shaded house, I tried the door, thinking
just to put my packages and note inside. In a moment a familiar
figure appeared at the door. Hemingway was wearing somewhat
tattered shorts, a sport shirt out at the waist, and no shoes. He asked
me in, and I introduced myself, handing him the package of film, the
wrapped bottle and the note, which he put on a table in the
entranceway. Politely, in the soft but high voice which surprised so,
coming from a man of his scale, he asked me to sit down, leading the
way into the spacious, informally furnished living room, along the
white plaster walls on which were low, overflowing bookcases. His
behavior was almost painfully shy. Motioning me to a deep chair
beside a tray groaning with bottles, he took one opposite. Apolo-
getically, he said that he was terribly hard at work, that it was going
well, and that he hadn't supposed that anything very good would
come of my calling on him. With a certain diffidence, he repeated his
familiar arguments about being unwilling to speak about writing, that
talking about it killed it, "took something from it," "made it go away,"
"spooked" him.

I assured him that I understood, but that we still wanted to record
him for the future. He demurred, and I asked him if he hadn't got
something from visiting and talking with established writers like
Sherwood Anderson when he was only an aspiring writer in Chicago,
before departing for France.

"Oh, but we never spoke of writing," replied Hemingway—pronouncing the word distinctively as if it were spelled *wright-ing*.
"Anderson told stories. He loved to tell stories, and he told them well.
But he wouldn't talk about writing; not then. It wouldn't have
worked. Later he was different. But I only saw him maybe four or
five times.

"You take Joyce. He would *never* talk about his writing. Oh,
maybe after he had finished something. *Ulysses*. He would explain
some of those things later. He would read aloud. He had a nice voice
and read well."

"Joyce had a beautiful tenor voice," I said.

"A nice voice," said Hemingway. "But if you came to talk about writing, he would only stare at you. He was nasty."

"He was rather cynical," I said.

"Not cynical. Nasty. But he was nice," said Hemingway.

He returned to the theme that he could not talk about his own work. He paused and looked at me over the tops of his steel-rimmed spectacles, his brown eyes pale and aged by time, and wind, and perhaps some of the things they had seen and he had done. "You see, I choke up when I talk about it. If I have to say anything, it has to be clearly written out." (The lengthy and perceptive interview subsequently published in *The Paris Review* was done with Hemingway carefully writing and rewriting many of his replies.)

"I have a little recording—perhaps the disc was pirated—" I said, "of your remarks to a radio correspondent upon the occasion of your notification of the Nobel Prize. You insisted then that writing was something that could not be done—at least by you—if you talked about it."

"That is public," said Hemingway. "It is what I would have said, if I had appeared for the award." Then, reflectively, he added, "I've lost so much time, 1940 to 1944, for instance, then that nonsense in Africa." He referred to the 1954 plane crash in which he was injured.

"The literary world is always speculating about the major book that you are supposed to have had in work for a long time," I said.

"I've got a bunch of stuff," Hemingway said obliquely, motioning to a room off the spacious living room.

I tried again. "Isn't this the big book that . . ."

"It's a novel," he cut in, "and I'm trying to finish it. I want to go to Spain and Africa." He paused and asked if I would have a drink. Guiltily, I rose and said that I felt like an interloper.

"No, no," he said. "I thought that you were my son Jack. I'd knocked off work. Stay a little while."

When I had sat down again, Hemingway inquired about my job, remarking that it must be a pretty good one. I told him something about it and, when he had asked me some more about myself, remarked that I was a journalist by trade and that I had kept a hand in, free lancing; that, in fact, he might be amused by a little feature I was assembling—on the ten greatest bars in the world—for *Esquire*.

"For *Esquire*? The ten greatest bars in the world?" Hemingway shook his head. "How could anybody work that out?" he asked, going right on. "Well, there's the Ritz, Paris; Harry's Bar, Venice; Costello's, New York; La Floridita here. The Floridita used to be nice. Open and airy with good cross-ventilation. But the bartenders are good. The food is good, too, but expensive. It's a nice place.

"Esquire," he said again. "I used to work for them. In the beginning for about two years. Gingrich, now the publisher, then the editor, came down and conned me. He's a pretty good con man." Then, with the courteous afterthought characteristic of him, Hemingway added, "A nice guy, too. They paid me $1,000 for "The Snows of Kilimanjaro."

"That was pretty good then, 1936," I said.

"Yes," Hemingway nodded agreeably, "but I was getting about a dollar a word then. Do you know how they used to get me? They used to print the cover and put me—my name—on it, then leave the form open. I'd have to fill it. That's how they got that ["The Snows of Kilimanjaro"]. What a con-man gimmick! But I don't feel bitter."

"Gingrich is a pretty keen fisherman," I said.

"I started him," said Hemingway. "But they do put out a pretty good book. I guess they call it that now, don't they?" he said, suddenly flashing that beacon-sized smile as if to signal our partnership in knowledge about this conceit of the magazine industry. "I keep up down here," he added, pointing at an elaborate magazine rack in the entrance hall of the house, which was filled with a large variety of periodicals.

Noticing a book—Jacques Maritain's *Reflections on America*—on the table behind the two slip-covered, old, over-stuffed chairs in which we sat, I remarked, "You may be happy to know . . ."

"My publisher sent it to me," he interjected, following my glance.

". . . that Jacques Maritain has steadily declined to let us film one of these conversations," I continued.

The big smile flashed again.

"There is an interview with you coming out in *The Paris Review*, isn't there?" I asked.

"Next month," he said, with some embarrassment. "George

Plimpton kept after me for three years. Finally I did it. It took me about five or six weeks. You have to be goddam sure what you're saying."

"I found a collection of those interviews in book form, *Writers at Work,* pretty interesting," I said.

"Yeah?" he said, warming up. "Some pretty good. But," he learned forward confidentially, "what a lot of bull----, too. How some of those guys can believe themselves. Jesus! But there is some pretty good stuff in that book. Simenon is good. We're lucky to have him. The way he writes, huh? All those books, and his saying that he doesn't know how they're going to turn out? How does he think anybody else writes? But when he talks about his *serious* books, his strong points, why they're just the wrong things—all the things wrong with Simenon. But when he just *writes,* he's good."

"Simenon's kind of a writing machine," I said.

"A writing machine," said Hemingway. "It all goes in, and it all comes out. And Dottie Parker," he murmured, apparently referring to the interview with her published in the same volume, but he didn't go on.

"I would have liked to have known her in the old *Vanity Fair* days," I said, "with Bob Benchley and Robert Sherwood. . . ."

"Bob Sherwood," Hemingway spoke the name, his voice dropping, barely audible, his gaze far away.

I felt myself for a moment like a sailor talking with the wind, but I went on. "There were some funny things developed in a few of those interviews. Isn't it funny how E. M. Forster, having been so analytical of writing, seemed himself to go out like a candle so long ago?"

"Yes, went out like a candle," Hemingway echoed again, his shaggy grey-white head bobbing assent. "Sure you can't have a drink?"

I stood up swiftly. "No, I feel bad coming by and taking up your time."

"No! Stay a while," he said. "I'm through working. I was just waiting for Jack. Have a drink."

"I will if you'll join me," I said.

"I'm having wine," he said.

"All right," I said. "That's fine by me."

Hemingway motioned toward the strong spirits on the tray beside me, and I shook my head. "May I excuse myself first?" I said, getting up.

He rose and directed me. I noticed the stand-up working place where he did his writing, the top of a bookcase near the double bed, supporting a reading board on which he usually writes, and a typewriter which he uses when he is working rapidly. The room also contained a large desk littered with newspapers, books and various gimcracks like any boy's or Franklin D. Roosevelt's, bar bells on the floor, some African trophies on the walls, a lesser kudu skin on the floor. Like everything about the house, his room had the air of long-lived-in, unpretentious comfort; it exhaled the immediate presence of an inhabitant who is at once literary and the man of action. Scribbled on the bathroom walls were numerous notations of diastolic and systolic blood pressures.

When I re-entered the living room, the host was returning with a bottle and ice: a large, high-shouldered man with the bulging calves of an athlete, thin ankles and big feet, lumbering forward, padding across the cool yellow tile floor. He served the wine and ice.

"Marques de Riscal," I said, recognizing the good Spanish red wine.

"Would you prefer sherry?" asked Hemingway courteously.

I said, "No," and he gave me ice and took some himself and we drank the red wine cool, as many Europeans do and as American wine pretenders abhor.

We talked of mutual friends and Venice, and I asked if there was any good shooting there that was public.

"It's not public, but I used to get a guide in Torcello, the last time was 1950, and we would work up the canals (those through the countryside) jump-shooting at passers."

"What are passers?" I asked.

The huge smile gleamed, then Hemingway laughed. "Any damn thing that flies by! They have many species that we have—teal, widgeon, pintails, some mallards, and, sure, geese, plenty of geese at the end."

We were talking of Africa and Spain when Hemingway paused and, speaking carefully, said: "The work is going pretty good. I get started at seven o'clock, have breakfast at about eight-thirty, get back to work at nine, stop for lunch and then hit it again after lunch. I'm

writing too much a day. Today, a thousand words. Too--------much.
I've got to hold myself down. But I'm trying to get finished. I want to
go to Spain and to Africa."

Taking up the conversation about Spain, Hemingway said, "I made
a documentary film once, myself—*The Spanish Earth,* 1937. I wrote
it, but Archie MacLeish and John Dos Passos were supposed to have
done it. I think I was a grip, too."

Since he had mentioned movies, I said, "Your work hasn't made
out too well in the movies for the most part."

"Jesus!" said Hemingway. "Usually I couldn't have anything to do
with the pictures, or didn't want to. The properties had usually been
sold or resold."

"*The Snows of Kilimanjaro* came out as a lot of hokum on the
screen," I said.

"My ex-wife had got that property," he said. "It was sold to
Hollywood long ago for something awfully small, and I never got
anything out of the picture or had anything to do with it. I have lent a
hand with *The Old Man and the Sea,* though, mostly trying to get the
big marlin, but even there didn't make out so well. I don't know."

By this time it was nearly dark. Hemingway had shown me about
and passed the time with great hospitality, and I felt that I had to
leave; besides I was anxious to put my journal in order. This time I
insisted on rising and walked into the entrance hall. Hemingway
protested kindly and followed me. He referred to the television
project that had brought me and said that primitive peoples believed
that if their pictures were taken they surrendered their personal
power, their *élan vital,* to those who possessed their images. (Hemingway was to write to me later: "I am superstitious about being
filmed or televised. Feel about it the way that certain tribes do and so
haven't done it, but good luck to you and to the other characters that
it does no harm to.")

I told him that I had encountered this belief among the people of
the outer Fiji Islands.

He smiled delightedly and clapped me on the shoulder. Then he
looked at me and said humorously, "You know that you can't buy
the principles of a lifetime with a bottle?"

"Read the note later on," I replied.

"Well, if anybody ever lands me for a filmed interview, it should be you," he said. "Maybe if I can get ahead, you know, like a pitcher gets ahead so that he can coast, maybe I'll do it. Or, if I get real bad. Oh, that's a stupid way to talk. Jeez, I'm sorry you brought this bottle. What is it?"

I told him.

"Jesus," said Hemingway. "I'll need an occasion."

"It's just from me to you with thanks, no strings," I said. "It won't go on the expense account. I came down here expressly to see you."

"I feel bad," he said. "But you're having some fun in town at night, I hope?"

"I've loved every minute of it," I said.

Hemingway seemed pleased to hear it, and, laughing, hand upon my shoulder, saw me to my waiting car. "I didn't mean what I said about Joyce," he said. "About coming to the door and just staring. Why don't you meet me at La Floridita tomorrow, mid-afternoon? Will it be all right if I bring something and write something in it?"

"Just please have a look at the Stravinsky film I've left you," I said. "He is pretty entertaining, and I think the television ordeal will look fairly painless, even fun."

"Yeah, he's a ham," said Hemingway, waving good-by.

By two-thirty the next afternoon I was installed at the bar of La Floridita, grateful for the cool quiet of the place and the majestic frozen daiquiri in my hand. (The drink was popularized there, and though they blend many kinds, the secret of their best is a teaspoonful of maraschino in the elixir.) I sat in the corner at the front beneath the bearded bronze bust of Ernest Hemingway.

After a while Papa and Miss Mary came in. Mrs. Hemingway had a daiquiri, and Hemingway asked for Scotch with a bit of crushed lemon and a little ice. Just then Hemingway's oldest son Jack (by his first wife, Hadley Richardson) came in. I found him to be an extremely attractive and affable chap. He had been living in Cuba for some time, and although his profession of stockbroker struck me as an improbable one for the son of Ernest Hemingway, I quickly realized he shared his father's interests in the outdoor life.

When Jack and Miss Mary became engaged in a splinter conversation, I told Hemingway that my own passion for trout fishing had begun with reading his two-part story, the *"Big Two-Hearted River,"* many years ago; that, in fact, while serving in the Navy in the

South Pacific, I had read and reread it (in *The Fifth Column and the First Forty-Nine Stories*) and had dreamed about the dark and quiet waters of the Michigan north country and young Nick Adams, alone, fishing for trout. I recalled how the exactly drawn atmosphere of the story had affected me, and how I had always wondered just why Hemingway had ended the second part of the story with Nick's dread of going into the dark swamp—"the fishing would be tragic. In the swamp fishing was a tragic adventure. Nick did not want it." I spoke the lines to him, there in La Floridita. I thought but did not remark how often the presence of tragedy hovered beyond the streams or bars of Hemingway's stories.

"Oh, that was just bait fishing," he said. "It doesn't really count as trout fishing." His voice and whole manner were suddenly embarrassed, I think, in trying not to appear affected, which he was, by his own words given back and the sincerity which was there, a suddenly tangible thing, between us after my doubtless terribly gauche reader-to-author remark.

My allusion to the Navy led Hemingway into several military observations, then literary ones. "There were a lot of good Navy books, I think. Of course *The Caine Mutiny* and a bunch of others, too, were——. What——, huh?"

He asked me what books about the last war I had liked and I mentioned *The Gallery* by John Horne Burns and Norman Mailer's *The Naked and the Dead*.

"Crap," he said. "Imagine a general not looking at the coordinates. He wouldn't last long. Mailer's was no real general. Crap." All this was said in the same quiet voice. Then, as I was to note his doing several times when he was moved to temper some harsh judgment, he added, "I ought to read it again. I might feel different, huh? You think it's good?"

Hemingway's modesty about many subjects that afternoon was at variance with tales told of him, but, although aware that this was scant acquaintance, I found it convincing enough. Not long before I had been talking with Van Wyck Brooks, the distinguished American literary historian, and he had said it seemed to him that Hemingway had never grown up, that he seemed permanently adolescent in his concern for "playing soldiers" and that in this respect he was perhaps typically American and, fine stylist though he was, he was less than

one of the greatest writers. Brooks had said something else, too,
about Robert Cohn, the touchy Jewish-American character of Hemingway's *The Sun Also Rises* (I cannot remember now what Brooks
said or precisely what I said to Hemingway on this point; certainly I
did not quote Brooks' remark, but I have noted down Hemingway's
rejoinder). I said something about Brooks and then something about
Cohn.

"Brooks thinks I'm a bum," commented Hemingway. "Well, if he
wants to call me a bum, that's all right. He's entitled to. He did good
work, huh? All that work about all those authors. But, Jesus Christ,
who made him—Cohn—say and stand for those things?" (Harold
Loeb, the author, has written that he was the original of Robert Cohn
and that Hemingway, rather too painfully for Loeb, pretty much put
him down on paper.)

The afternoon was waning, drinks came and went, but Hemingway partook sparingly of his special mix. I found the chance to return
to the topic of the "big book."

"Look," he said, "what I have written is my family's money in the
bank. Supposing I was to publish everything I had. Imagine what it
would do to taxes! I've got some stuff put away."

I asked him whether *The Old Man and the Sea* was the book
about "the sea, about life" which he had been reported to have been
working on over a period of time.

"Hell, no," he said. "You're talking about the big one, about war,
about life." He leaned close over the bar. "I had blood poisoning
when I wrote *The Old Man*. I wrote it right off in a few weeks. I wrote
it for a dame; she didn't think I had it left in me. I guess I showed her.
I hope so. There was a woman behind each of my books."

I was startled by his apparent candor, but maybe the whole
afternoon at the long bar, the big frozen daiquiris sliding down
leaving a numbness for a minute had something to do with my
passive mood. Hemingway said a few other things that shocked me;
he spoke with bitterness about one of his family, but even then he
spoke in a tone of reason, the more troubling for its conviction.
Hemingway clearly loved talking, but he didn't *make* talk, and I have
wondered since if he meant to shock, took any pleasure in it; I didn't
think so then.

Miss Mary gently interrupted our discourse to suggest that perhaps they should be getting back to the finca. Hemingway took out of an envelope a copy of a fine English edition of *The Old Man and the Sea,* beautifully illustrated with drawings by C. F. Tunnicliffe and Raymond Sheppard. Inside the flyleaf he had inscribed a friendly note. I was touched and grateful, but when I tried to thank him he busied himself with the bartender, having two large drinks prepared for the ride back to his farm. Then we all made our farewells and he and Miss Mary went out to their open car, to sit up in the back seat and be chauffeured out to the country, drinks in hand.

Jack had gone off and I stayed on a while, finishing my drink.

"That's quite a guy," a young U.S. airman said, and I replied, "That's the truth," and hurried back to my writing table.

Hemingway and I talked again briefly, in New York. In the Autumn of 1959, from Spain, where he was once more following the bulls, Hemingway wrote, "Take care of yourself so we can have another drink at La Floridita." I wish it could have been that way.

An Afternoon with Hemingway
Edward Stafford/1964

Reprinted from *Writer's Digest*, 44 (December 1964), 18–22.

Havana was still free that summer—and hot, as it will always be.
They still served you frozen daiquiris during the wait for customs at
the airport. Castro was a remote shadow in the eastern mountains,
and Ernest Hemingway was still alive and working.

Papa lived and worked at his Finca Vigia in the suburb of San
Francisco de Paulo. It was necessary to stop at the gate just off the
main road and get an old man who lived nearby to open it. Then
there was a straight road through the woods for perhaps a quarter-
mile, a curve to the left—and the Finca. It had broad steps, columns
and a feeling of spaciousness, informality and comfort. It was of not
recently painted white stucco, un-air-conditioned and a little over-
grown. From the back there was a view of the rooftops of Havana
with the sea beyond; there was a rectangular pool where each day
Mary Hemingway swam her mile, in the nude for freedom of
movement, and fired the gardener if he watched. A few yards from
the house, but matching it in materials and appearance, was the
squarish, three-story tower in the top of which Hemingway did his
writing. There were also cats—about fifteen, mostly kittens, which
lived in the tower's first floor—the "cat house."

Inside, the Finca was laid out like a short-legged H—a long living
room capped by smaller ones at its ends. One of the smaller rooms
was a den/office/library, another a dining room, another a library. The
first was the most interesting, with an incredibly piled and cluttered
desk, heads of buffalo and Kudu high on the walls, two zebra-
covered scrapbooks of Hemingway obituaries published prematurely
at the time of his double plane crash in Africa over three and a half
years before, and books. Everywhere, in all rooms, there were books.
A writer, Papa believed, had to read, for pleasure, for knowledge, for
experience, but most importantly, to see what the competition is.

"There is no use," he said, "writing anything that has been written

before unless you can beat it. What a writer has to do is write what
hasn't been written before or beat dead men at what they have
done." Only dead men are useful as standards, as competitors,
because only their work has been tested by time and has proven
value. "It is like a miler running against the clock rather than simply
against whoever is in the race with him. Unless he runs against time,
he will never know what he is capable of attaining."

Papa picked his dead milers with discrimination. On his shelves
were books by Tolstoi, Dostoevsky, Stendhal, De Maupassant, Mann,
Joyce, W. H. Hudson, George Moore, Stephen Crane, Turgenev,
Flaubert, and several dozen others, similarly disparate as to era and
nationality, having in common only their greatness.

Perhaps it was my knowledge of his lifetime of artistic discipline
and integrity, whatever his personal problems and foibles, and of his
single-minded, undeviating search for his own conception of literary
perfection, which prejudiced me in advance, but, for whatever
reason, his own greatness seemed immediately apparent.

White-bearded, wearing a long, white, Cuban shirt, he came down
the front steps with "Miss Mary" to greet us. I had recently achieved
brief attention as a successful contestant on a television quiz show by
answering (without assistance) a series of questions on American
literature, a number of which had concerned Ernest Hemingway; and
I had unashamedly made use of my moment of glory to arrange a
meeting with him. During the introductions Hemingway was warm
and cordial, his handshake strong and good, but he wasted no
words, made no small talk.

I had been secretly a little worried, despite my enthusiasm for his
writing, that Ernest Hemingway, the man, would be given to the sort
of brusque, Anglo-Saxon dialog that is found in his books, and,
although after a decade and a half at sea and ashore in the Navy, I
could speak and understand this language as well as any, I have
never been a man for four letter words in mixed company and I
knew that my liberal but convent-bred wife would be in agony—and
I with her. My worrying could not have been more groundless.
Whatever he may have been in other times and at other places (and I
doubt if he were very different) the Hemingway who talked with us in
the long living room of the Finca Vigia was candid and direct but a

kind and hospitable gentleman to whom it would have been incon-
ceivable to offend a guest in his home.

Naturally I was interested in talking about Hemingway and his
work. He was not. He was interested in me and my experiences on
the quiz show and the sort of questions that were asked—which
brought us onto common ground with a discussion of the Hemingway questions. As I talked, his level brown eyes never left my fact. He
listened completely, concentrated fully with an absolute lack of self-
consciousness, without thinking of what he was going to say next;
and when I was through, he gave me back, with utter candor,
whatever response had been elicited in the clear, cool mind behind
those eyes.

Papa enjoyed hearing the questions that had been asked about his
work, and answering them himself, slowly, thoughtfully; thinking back
and relating events to each other.

What two plays had he written and what were their dates of
publication?

The Fifth Column was easy because he remembered well writing it
during the late fall of '36 and early winter of '37 in Hotel Florida in
Madrid which was being hit repeatedly by Franco's artillery. It took
longer to remember when the little three page *Today is Friday* was
published but he thought back, logically, and got it.

We had drinks which Miss Mary mixed. Papa was on the wagon,
except for light wine, since the African crashes.

What book had he published in October of 1926 and what was its
English title?

Papa remembered there had been two books that year; that
Torrents of Spring had come out, appropriately, in the spring and that
left *The Sun Also Rises* for October. In England it was called *Fiesta*.

We discussed the sources of the titles of *The Sun Also Rises, A
Farewell to Arms, For Whom the Bell Tolls,* and *Across the River and
Into the Trees,* then the nationalities of the heroines (English, Scotch,
Spanish and Italian) which had been other questions, and finally
turned to the subject I most wanted to develop—Hemingway's
thoughts on the profession in which he had made himself a giant, to
which he had given his life and all his great energy and talent—
writing.

My wife needled him. "Is it true," she asked, "that you take a
pitcher of martinis up into the tower every morning when you go up
to write?"

"Jeezus Christ!" Papa was incredulous. "Have you ever heard of
anyone who drank while he worked? You're thinking of Faulkner. He
does sometimes—and I can tell right in the middle of a page when
he's had his first one. Besides," he added, "who in hell would mix
more than one martini at a time, anyway?"

Having been guilty of that heresy any number of times, but
recognizing his mastery in this field also, I let the question remain
rhetorical.

I had just begun work on a biography of an aircraft carrier which
had had a distinguished career in the Second World War and I was
very seriously interested in the trade of writing, the nuts and bolts, the
mechanics, and I knew I would never have another chance like this to
learn from one of the great professionals of all time.

"What about hours?" I asked. "How long can you actually be
productive on a daily basis? How do you know when to stop?"

"That's something you have to learn about yourself. The important
thing is to work every day. I work from about seven until about noon.
Then I go fishing or swimming, or whatever I want. The best way is
always to stop when you are going good. If you do that you'll never
be stuck. And don't think or worry about it until you start to write
again the next day. That way your subconscious will be working on it
all the time, but if you worry about it, your brain will get tired before
you start again. But work every day. No matter what has happened
the day or night before, get up and bite on the nail."

This was the kind of thing I had come to Havana to hear.

I became more specific, "I was never in the *Enterprise*," (the
carrier my book was about) I confessed. "I'm not sure I've ever seen
her except maybe once, at sea, several miles away. Is that going to
hurt the book?"

"Have you been on other carriers?"

"Yes."

"O.K. Then I'm glad you weren't aboard the *Enterprise*. If you've
been in a street fight in one block, one city, you can write about a
street fight in another block or city. And if you had been aboard, you
would have been in a particular department or unit and it would be

hard not to write from the viewpoint of that unit, or over-emphasize it or the people in it.

"But," he went on, "It's getting kind of late to write about World War II. Timing is important. At first it is too fresh and you are too close to it, then there is no good time to write, and after that it begins to get too far away."

I thought about that and said I felt I could still write about that war. I remembered it well, I had kept a careful journal to help the memory, and I had been in almost all the places and several of the actions in which the carrier had been.

That was important, Papa said, because one of the things you had to have to write was an exact, detailed and specific knowledge of what you were writing about. The other "absolute necessities," he said, were "a real seriousness in regard to writing, and talent."

I thought that in this case I had the first two and would find out shortly if I had the third. But I wanted to know more of the mechanics.

"What about the very first draft?" I asked him. "How do you do it? Pencil, pen, typewriter, dictation? How?"

"When you write," he said, "Your object is to convey every sensation, sight, feeling, emotion, to the reader. So you have to work over what you write. If you use a pencil, you get three different views of it to see if you are getting it across the way you want to. First, when you read it over, then when it is typed, and again in proof. And it keeps it fluid longer so that you can improve it easier."

"How do you ever learn to convey every sensation, sight and feeling to the reader? Just keep working at it for forty-odd years the way you have? Are there any tricks?"

"No. The hardest trade in the world to do is the writing of straight, honest prose about human beings. But there are ways you can train yourself."

"How?"

"When you walk into a room and you get a certain feeling or emotion, remember back until you see exactly what it was that gave you the emotion. Remember what the noises and smells were and what was said. Then write it down, making it clear so the reader will see it too and have the same feeling you had. And watch people, observe, try to put yourself in somebody else's head. If two men argue, don't just think who is right and who is wrong. Think what both their sides are. As a man, you know who is right and who is wrong; you have to judge. As a writer, you should not judge, you should understand."

I felt as though I were monopolizing the conversation and I wasn't even sure Papa was enjoying it, though he seemed to be and was talking earnestly. But there was so much I wanted to know.

"Is it a good thing to talk over your work with other people, other writers? Is that a way to learn? It has often seemed to me that most of the great talents of the century were living in Paris in the 20's when you were, and you all knew each other. You must have talked about writing—and it must have helped."

"Good conversation with good people is always stimulating, especially *after* work. You can talk about writing generally, about words, and when you are learning and trust or respect anothr writer, he can help with the blue pencil and in other ways—but never talk about a story you are working on. If you tell it, you never write it. You spoil the freshness, you mouth it up and get rid of it in the telling instead of the writing. Writers should work alone, *then* talk."

In the course of the talking we had lunch. I remember a delicious cold soup made with lots of vegetables and clear water which Miss Mary explained was an Andulasian peasant dish. It was perfect for the hot climate.

The talk turned to other writers. My wife proposed and defended Graham Greene whom Papa good naturedly thought was "a jerk" because he "traded on his religion" and was a convert. It was bad enough, he thought, for a woman to be converted, but for a man, it was unforgivable. But, as if to prove his lack of bitterness, he went to the library and came back with a copy of Greene's latest book and the only one my wife had not read, and inscribed it for her: "From her friend, Ernie (Graham) Greenway." Kathleen Winsor he did not consider a professional writer. Alan Moorehead, in Papa's opinion, was great. He insisted that I read *Gallipoli* which I said I would do, but that was not enough.

"Don't just say that," he said, holding me with his eyes across the table. "Really get it and read it!"

In his humility, he was not aware that any apprentice writer like myself needed no such urging when he recommended a book. It was already branded onto my memory and, of course, I would read it.

During lunch, and when the strangeness had worn off a little, Miss Mary, in her forthright way, chastised me gently for having addressed Papa as "Ernest" in the letter I had written him before our visit. I tried lamely, if truthfully, to explain that I had considered any number of salutations before using that one but that no other seemed right; and that, probably, the wrong one seemed right because of my long familiarity with everything he had written and which had been written about him. I wasn't making very much sense when Papa cut in.

"Oh, hell. It was one writer to another!"

Like a Sunday duffer to Sammy Sneed! It was a generous compliment.

When the time came to leave, it was still hot and humid, with no breeze. The sweat glistened on all our faces and emphasized the old bullet groove on the left side of Papa's forehead. Miss Mary walked us out to the car and we were both in when my wife missed her purse. I went back for it, and was turning to leave again when I saw Hemingway, solid, scarred, grizzled and completely naked at the other end of the living room. It was hot and his guests had left. We grinned at each other and I ducked out, glad it was I and not my wife who had returned.

We exchanged cards and notes and I sent him the first chapters of the carrier book, but I did not see Papa again. Yet, like many others, whatever I write, if it is well and truly written, will be partly his.

Hemingway in Cuba

Robert Manning/1965

Reprinted, by permission of Robert Manning, from the *Atlantic Monthly,* 216 (August 1965), 101–108.

On the shore of Havana's back harbor a stubborn hulk rests in drydock and erodes with time. Its engine and expensive fishing tackle are gone. The fading letters of its name, *Pilar,* are still visible on the stern. "No one else should sail the *Pilar,*" says Mary Hemingway. She had hoped to have it towed to sea and sunk off the port of Cojimar, deep into the fishing hole where a strike came at last to the old man "who fished alone in the Gulf Stream and had gone eighty-four days now without taking a fish." The Cuban government's red tape prevented that, so the *Pilar* now decays in the Caribbean sun.

Ten miles from Havana, in the village of San Francisco de Paula, is Hemingway's longtime home away from home. The plantation he called Finca Vigia (Lookout Farm), with its big limestone villa and thirteen acres of banana trees, tropical shrubs, and casual gardens, stands much as he and his wife left it in 1960 when he came home to the States for the last time. It is now a Cuban government museum. Some Cubans who ran the place for "Papa" still live and work there, caring for the grounds and the sprawling villa and pointing out to visitors the pool where "Papa" swam, the big bedroom where he wrote, and the tall white tower where he would sit to work or to stare from his heights toward the spread of Havana.

Who in my generation was not moved by Hemingway the writer and fascinated by Hemingway the maker of his own legend? "Veteran out of the wars before he was twenty," as Archibald MacLeish described him. "Famous at twenty-five; thirty a master." Wine-stained moods in the sidewalk cafés and roistering nights in Left Bank *boîtes.* Walking home alone in the rain. Talk of death, and scenes of it, in the Spanish sun. Treks and trophies in Tanganyika's green hills. Duck-shooting in the Venetian marshes. Fighting in, and writing about, two world wars. Loving and drinking and fishing out of Key

West and Havana. Swaggering into Toots Shor's or posturing in *Life* magazine or talking a verbless sort of Choctaw for the notebooks of Lillian Ross and the pages of the *New Yorker.*

By the time I got the opportunity to meet him, he was savoring the highest moment of his fame—he had just won the Nobel Prize for Literature—but he was moving into the twilight of his life. He was fifty-five but looked older, and was trying to mend a ruptured kidney, a cracked skull, two compressed and one cracked vertebra, and bad burns suffered in the crash of his airplane in the Uganda bush the previous winter. Those injuries, added to half a dozen head wounds, more than 200 shrapnel scars, a shot-off kneecap, wounds in the feet, hands, and groin, had slowed him down. The casually comfortable Cuban villa had become more home than any place he'd had, and days abroad the *Pilar* were his substitute for high adventure abroad.

In a telephone conversation between San Francisco de Paula and New York, Hemingway had agreed to be interviewed on the occasion of his Nobel award, but he resisted at first because one of the magazines I worked with had recently published a penetrating article on William Faulkner. "You guys cut him to pieces, to pieces," Hemingway said. "No, it was a good piece," I said, "and it would have been even better if Faulkner had seen the writer."

"Give me a better excuse," Hemingway said, and then thought of one himself. He saw the arrival of a visitor as an opportunity to fish on the *Pilar* after many weeks of enforced idleness. "Bring a heavy sweater, and we'll go out on the boat," he said. "I'll explain to Mary that you're coming down to cut me up and feed me to William Faulkner."

A handsome young Cuban named René, who had grown up on Hemingway's place as his all-round handyman, chauffeur, and butler, was at Havana Airport to meet me and hustle my luggage, which included a batch of new phonograph records and, as a last-minute addition, a gift from Marlene Dietrich. On hearing that someone was going to Cuba to see her old friend, she sent along a newly released recording called "Shake, Rattle, and Roll," which now may be vaguely remembered as the Java man artifact in the evolution of popular rock 'n' roll. "Just like the Kraut," said Hemingway. He found the sentiment more appealing than the music.

A big man. Even after allowing for all the descriptions and photographs, the first impression of Hemingway in the flesh was size. He was barefoot and barelegged, wearing only floppy khaki shorts and a checked sport shirt, its tail tumbling outside. He squinted slightly through round silver-framed glasses, and a tentative smile, the sort that could instantly turn into a sneer or snarl, showed through his clipped white beard. Idleness had turned him to paunch, and he must have weighed then about 225 pounds, but there was no other suggestion of softness in the burly, broad-shouldered frame, and he had the biceps and calves of an N.F.L. linebacker.

"Drink?" Hemingway asked. The alacrity of the reply pleased him, and the smile broadened into a laugh. He asked René to mix martinis and said, "Thank God you're a drinking man. I've been worried ever since I told you to come down. There was a photographer here for three days a while ago who didn't drink. He was the cruelest man I've ever met. Cruelest man in the world. Made us stand in the sun for hours at a time. And he didn't drink." With still caution, he sank into a large overstuffed chair which had been lined back, sides, and bottom with big art and picture books to brace his injured back.

Hemingway sipped and said, "Now, if you find me talking in monosyllables or without any verbs, you tell me, because I never really talk that way. She [he meant Lillian Ross] told me she wanted to write a piece of homage to Hemingway. That's what she told me when I agreed to see her up in New York." He laughed. "I knew her for a long time. Helped her with her first big piece, on Sidney Franklin.

"I don't mind talking tonight," Hemingway said, "because I never work at night. There's a lot of difference between night thinking and day thinking. Night thoughts are usually nothing. The work you do at night you always will have to do over again in the daytime anyhow. So let's talk. When I talk, incidentally, it's just talk. But when I write I mean it for good."

The living room was nearly fifty feet long and high-ceilinged, with gleaming white walls that set off the Hemingway's small but choice collection of paintings (including a Miró, two Juan Gris, a Klee, a Braque—since stolen from the villa—and five André Massons), a few trophy heads from the African safaris. In another room, near the entrance to a large tile-floored dining room, was an oil portrait of

Hemingway in his thirties, wearing a flowing, open-collar white shirt. "It's an old-days picture of me as Kid Balzac by Waldo Pierce," said Hemingway. "Mary has it around because she likes it."

He rubbed the tight-curled white beard and explained that he wore it because when clean-shaven his skin was afflicted with sore spots if he spent much time in the sun. "I'll clip the damned thing off for Christmas so as not to run against Santa Claus," he said, "and if I rest the hide a couple of weeks at a time, I may be able to keep it off. Hope so anyway."

In one large corner of the living room stood a six-foot-high rack filled with dozens of magazines and newspapers from the States, London, and Paris. In casual piles, books littered windowsills and tables and spilled a trail into two large rooms adjacent. One was a thirty-by-twenty-foot library whose floor-to-ceiling shelves sagged with books. The other was Hemingway's large but crowded bedroom study— littered with correspondence in varied stages of attention or neglect. There were neat piles of opened letters together with stamped and addressed replies; cardboard boxes overflowing with the shards of correspondence that had been opened, presumably read, and one day might be filed; a couple of filing cabinets, whose mysteries probably were best known to a part-time stenographer the Heming-ways brought in from Havana a day or two at a time when needed. There was also a large lionskin, in the gaping mouth of which lay half a dozen letters and a pair of manila envelopes. "That's the Urgent in-box," Hemingway explained.

The villa seemed awash with books—nearly 400, including two dozen cookbooks, in Mary Hemingway's bedroom; more than 500, mostly fiction, history, and music, in the big sitting room; another 300, mostly French works of history and fiction, in an elegantly tiled room called the Venetian Room; nearly 2000 in the high-shelved library, these carefully divided into history, military books, biography, geography, natural history, some fiction, and a large collection of maps; 900 volumes, mostly military manuals and textbooks, history and geography in Spanish, and sports volumes, in Hemingway's bedroom. In the tall tower he kept another 400 volumes, including foreign editions of his own works, and some 700 overflowed into shelves and tabletops in the finca's small guesthouse. All the books, including Hemingway's collection of autographed works by many of his contemporaries, were impounded at the villa by the Castro regime, though Mrs. Hemingway was able to take away some of the paintings and personal belongings.

From the kitchen came sounds and smells of dinner in preparation. René emerged with two bottles of a good Bordeaux from a cellar that was steadily replenished from France and Italy. Evening sounds grew strident in the soft tropical outdoors. Distant dogs yelped. Near the house, a hoot owl broke into short, sharp cries. "That's the Bitchy Owl," Hemingway said. "He'll go on like that all night. He's lived here longer than we have."

"I respect writing very much," he said abruptly, "the writer not at all, except as the instrument to do the writing. When a writer retires deliberately from life or is forced out of it by some defect, his writing has a tendency to atrophy, just like a man's limb when it's not used."

"I'm not advocating the strenuous life for everyone or trying to say it's the choice form of life. Anyone who's had the luck or misfortune to be an athlete has to keep his body in shape. The body and mind are closely coordinated. Fattening of the body can lead to fattening of the mind. I would be tempted to say that it can lead to fattening of the soul, but I don't know anything about the soul." He halted, broodingly, as if reflecting on his own aches and pains, his too ample paunch, a blood pressure that was too high, and a set of muscles that were suffering too many weeks of disuse. "However, in everyone the process of fattening or wasting away will set in, and I guess one is as bad as the other."

He had been reading about medical discoveries which suggested to him that a diet or regimen or treatment that may work for one man does not necessarily work for another. "This was known years ago, really, by people who make proverbs. But now doctors have discovered that certain men need more exercise than others; that certain men are affected by alcohol more than others; that certain people can assimilate more punishment in many ways than others.

"Take Primo Carnera, for instance. Now he was a real nice guy, but he was so big and clumsy it was pitiful. Or take Tom Wolfe, who just never could discipline his mind to his tongue. Or Scott Fitzgerald, who just couldn't drink." He pointed to a couch across the room. "If Scott had been drinking with us and Mary called us to dinner, Scott'd make it to his feet, all right, but then he'd probably fall down. Alcohol was just poison to him. Because all these guys had these weaknesses, it won them sympathy and favor, more sometimes than a guy without these defects would get."

For a good part of his adult life Hemingway was, of course, a ten-goal drinker, and he could hold it well. He was far more disciplined in this regard, though, than the legend may suggest. Frequently when he was working hard, he would drink nothing, except perhaps a glass or two of wine with meals. By rising at about daybreak or half an hour thereafter, he had put in a full writing day by ten or eleven in the morning and was ready for relaxation when others were little more than under way.

As in his early days, Hemingway in the late years worked with painful slowness. He wrote mostly in longhand, frequently while standing at a bookcase in his bedroom; occasionally he would typewrite ("when trying to keep up with dialogue"). For years he carefully logged each day's work. Except for occasional spurts when he was engaged in relatively unimportant efforts, his output ran between 400 and 700 words a day. Mary Hemingway remembers very few occasions when it topped 1000 words.

He did not find writing to be quick or easy. "I always hurt some," he remarked.

Hemingway was capable of great interest in and generosity toward younger writers and some older writers, but as he shows in *A Moveable Feast* (written in 1957–1959 and finished in the spring of 1961), he had a curious and unbecoming compulson to poke and peck at the reputations of many of his literary contemporaries. Gertrude Stein, Sherwood Anderson, T. S. Eliot, not to mention Fitzgerald, Wolfe, Ford Madox Ford, James Gould Cozzens, and others, were invariably good for a jab or two if their names came up. As for the critics—"I often feel," he said, "that there is now a rivalry between writing and criticism, rather than the feeling that one should help the other." Writers today could not learn much from the critics. "Critics should deal more with dead writers. A living writer can learn a lot from dead writers."

Fiction-writing, Hemingway felt, was to invent out of knowledge. "To invent out of knowledge means to produce inventions that are true. Every man should have a built-in automatic crap detector operating inside him. It also should have a manual drill and crank handle in case the machine breaks down. If you're going to write, you have to find out what's bad for you. Part of that you learn fast, and then you learn what's good for you."

What sort of things? "Well, take certain diseases. These diseases are not good for you. I was born before the age of antibiotics, of course. . . . Now take *The Big Sky* [by A. B. Guthrie]. That was a very good book in many ways, and it was very good on one of the diseases . . . just about the best book ever written on the clap." Hemingway smiled.

"But back to inventing. In *The Old Man and the Sea* I knew two or three things about the situation, but I didn't know the story." He hesitated, filling the intervals with a vague movement of his hands. "I didn't even know if that big fish was going to bite for the old man when it started smelling around the bait. I had to write on, inventing out of knowledge. You reject everything that is not or can't be completely true. I didn't know what was going to happen for sure in *For Whom the Bell Tolls* or *Farewell to Arms*. I was inventing."

Philip Young's *Ernest Hemingway,* published in 1953, had attributed much of Hemingway's inspiration or "invention" to his violent experiences as a boy and in World War I.

"If you haven't read it, don't bother," Hemingway volunteered. "How would you like it if someone said that everything you've done in your life was done because of some trauma. Young had a theory that was like—you know, the Procrustean bed, and he had to cut me to fit into it."

During dinner, the talk continued on writing styles and techniques. Hemingway thought too many contemporary writers defeated themselves through addiction to symbols. "No good book has ever been written that has in it symbols arrived at beforehand and stuck in." He waved a chunk of French bread. "That kind of symbol sticks out like—like raisins in raisin bread. Raisin bread is all right, but plain bread is better."

He mentioned Santiago, his old fisherman, in roughly these terms: Santiago was never alone because he had his friend and enemy, the sea, and the things that lived in the sea, some of which he loved and others he hated. He loved the sea, but the sea is a great whore, as the book made clear. He had tried to make everything in the story real— the boy, the sea, and the marlin and the sharks, the hope being that each would then mean many things. In that way, the parts of a story become symbols, but they are not first designed or planted as symbols.

The Bitchy Owl hooted the household to sleep. I was awakened by tropical birds at the dawn of a bright and promising day. This was to be Hemingway's first fishing trip on *Pilar* since long before his African crash. By six thirty he was dressed in yesterday's floppy shorts and sport shirt, barefooted, and hunched over his New York *Times*, one of the six papers he and Mary read every day. From the record player came a mixture of Scarlatti, Beethoven, Oscar Peterson, and a remake of some 1928 Louis Armstrong.

At brief intervals Hemingway popped a pill into his mouth. "Since the crash I have to take so many of them they have to fight among themselves unless I space them out," he said.

While we were breakfasting, a grizzled Canary Islander named Gregorio, who served as the *Pilar's* first mate, chef, caretaker, and bartender, was preparing the boat for a day at sea. By nine o'clock, with a young nephew to help him, he had fueled the boat, stocked it with beer, whiskey, wine, and a bottle of tequila, a batch of fresh limes, and food for a large seafood lunch afloat. As we made out of Havana Harbor, Gregorio at the wheel and the young boy readying the deep-sea rods, reels, and fresh bait-fish, Hemingway pointed out landmarks and waved jovially to passing skippers. They invariably waved back, occasionally shouting greetings to "Papa." He sniffed the sharp sea air with delight and peered ahead for the dark line made by the Gulf Stream. "Watch the birds," he said. "They show us when the fish are up."

Mary Hemingway had matters to handle at the finca and in the city, so she could not come along, but out of concern for Heming- way's health she exacted a promise. In return for the long-missed fun of a fishing expedition, he agreed to take it easy and to return early, in time for a nap before an art exhibit to which he and Mary had promised their support. He was in a hurry, therefore, to reach good fishing water. Gregorio pushed the boat hard to a strech of the Gulf Stream off Cojimar. Hemingway relaxed into one of the two cushioned bunks in the boat's open-ended cabin.

"It's wonderful to get out on the water. I need it." He gestured toward the ocean. "It's the last free place there is, the sea. Even Africa's about gone; it's at war, and that's going to go on for a very long time."

The *Pilar* fished two rods from its high antenna-like outriggers and two from seats at the stern, and at Hemingway's instruction, Gregorio and the boy baited two with live fish carefully wired to the hooks, and two with artificial lures. A man-o'-war bird gliding lazily off the coast pointed to the first school of the day, and within an hour the *Pilar* had its first fish, a pair of bonito sounding at the end of the outrigger lines. Before it was over, the day was to be one of the best fishing days in many months, with frequent good runs of bonito and dolphin and pleasant interludes of quiet in which to sip drinks, to soak up the Caribbean sun, and to talk.

Sometimes moody, sometimes erupting with boyish glee at the strike of a tuna or the golden blue explosion of a hooked dolphin, and sometimes—as if to defy or outwit his wounds—pulling himself by his arms to the flying bridge to steer the *Pilar* for a spell, Hemingway talked little of the present, not at all of the future, and a great deal of the past.

He recalled when Scribner's sent him first galley proofs of *For Whom the Bell Tolls.* "I remember, I spent ninety hours on the proofs of that book without once leaving the hotel room. When I finished, I thought the type was so small nobody would ever buy the book. I'd shot my eyes, you see. I had corrected the manuscript several times but still was not satisfied. I told Max Perkins about the type, and he said if I really thought it was too small, he'd have the whole book reprinted. That's a real expensive thing, you know. He was a sweet guy. But Max was right, the type was all right."

"Do you ever read any of your stuff over again?"

"Sometimes I do," he said. "When I'm feeling low. It makes you feel good to look back and see you can write."

"Is there anything you've written that you would do differently if you could do it over?"

"Not yet."

New York. "It's a very unnatural place to live. I could never live
there. And there's not much fun going to the city now. Max is dead.
Granny Rice is dead. He was a wonderful guy. We always used to go
to the Bronx Zoo and look at the animals."

The Key West days, in the early thirties, were a good time. "There
was a fighter there—he'd had one eye ruined, but he was still pretty
good, and he decided to start fighting again. He wanted to be his
own promoter. He asked me if I would referee his bout each week. I
told him, 'Nothing doing,' he shouldn't go in the ring anymore. Any
fighter who knew about his bad eye would just poke his thumb in the
other one and then beat his head off.

"The fighter said, 'The guys come from somewhere else won't
know 'bout my eye, and no one around here in the Keys gonna dare
poke my eye.'

"So I finally agreed to referee for him. This was the Negro section,
you know, and they really introduced me: 'And the referee for
tonight, the world-famous millionaire, sportsman, and playboy, Mister
Ernest Hemingway!' " Hemingway chuckled. "Playboy was the greatest title they thought they could give a man." Chuckle again. "How
can the Nobel Prize move a man who has heard plaudits like that?"

Frequently a sharp cry from Gregorio on the flying bridge interrupted the talk. "Feesh! Papa, feesh!" Line would snap from one of
the outriggers, and a reel begin to snarl. "You take him," Hemingway
would say, or if two fish struck at once, as frequently happened, he
would leap to one rod and I to the other.

For all the hundreds of times it had happened to him, he still
thrilled with delight at the quivering run of a bonito or the slash of a
dolphin against the sky. "Ah, beautiful! A beautiful fish. Take him
softly now. Easy. Easy. Work him with style. That's it. Rod up slowly.
Now reel in fast. *Suave! Suave!* Don't break his mouth. If you jerk,
you'll break his mouth, and the hook will go."

When action lulled, he would scan the seascape for clues to better
spots. Once a wooden box floated in the near distance, and he
ordered Gregorio toward it. "We'll fish that box," he said, explaining
that small shrimp seek shelter from the sun beneath flotsam or
floating patches of seaweed and these repositories of food attract
dolphin. At the instant the lures of the stern rods passed the box, a
dolphin struck and was hooked, to be pumped and reeled in with the

heavy-duty glass rod whose butt rested in a leather rod holder strapped around the hips.

He talked about the act of playing a fish as if it were an English sentence. "The way to do it, the style, is not just an idle concept. It is simply the way to get done what is supposed to be done; in this case it brings in the fish. The fact that the right way looks pretty or beautiful when it's done is just incidental."

Hemingway had written only one play, *The Fifth Column*. Why no others?

"If you write a play, you have to stick around and fix it up," he said. "They always want to fool around with them to make them commercially successful, and you don't like to stick around that long. After I've written, I want to go home and take a shower."

Almost absently, he plucked James Joyce out of the air. "Once Joyce said to me he was afraid his writing was too suburban and that maybe he should get around a bit and see the world, the way I was doing. He was under great discipline, you know—his wife, his work, his bad eyes. And his wife said, yes, it *was* too suburban. 'Jim could do with a spot of that lion-hunting.' How do you like that? A *spot* of lion-hunting!

"We'd go out, and Joyce would fall into an argument or a fight. He couldn't even see the man, so he'd say. 'Deal with him, Hemingway! Deal with him!' " Hemingway paused. "In the big league it is not the way it says in the books."

Hemingway was not warm toward T. S. Eliot. He preferred to praise Ezra Pound, who at that time was still confined in St. Elizabeth's mental hospital in Washington. "Ezra Pound is a great poet, and whatever he did, he has been punished greatly, and I believe should be freed to go and write poems in Italy, where he is loved and understood. He was the master of Eliot. I was a member of an organization which Pound founded with Natalia Barney in order to get Eliot out of his job in a bank so he could be free to write poetry. It was called Bel Esprit. Eliot, I believe, was able to get out of his job and edit a review and write poetry freely due to the backing of other people than this organization. But the organization was typical of Pound's generosity and interest in all forms of the arts regardless of any benefits to himself or of the possibilities that the people he encouraged would be his rivals.

"Eliot is a winner of the Nobel Prize. I believe it might well have gone to Pound, as a poet. Pound certainly deserved punishment, but I believe this would be a good year to release poets and allow them to continue to write poetry. . . . Ezra Pound, no matter what he may think, is not as great a poet as Dante, but he is a very great poet for all his errors."

Dusk was coming when the *Pilar* turned toward Havana Harbor, its skipper steering grandly from the flying bridge. What remained of the bottle of tequila and a half of lime rested in a holder cut into the mahogany rail near the wheel. "To ward off sea serpents," Hemingway explained, passing the bottle for a ceremonial homecoming swig.

At the docks, René reported that the gallery opening had been postponed. Hemingway was overjoyed. "Now we can relax for a while and then get some sleep. We went out and had a good day and got pooped. Now we can sleep."

Hemingway's good spirits on his return helped to diminish his wife's concern about his overextending himself. She served up a hot oyster stew, and later, clutching an early nightcap, Hemingway sprawled with pleased fatigue in his big armchair and talked of books he had recently read. He had started Saul Bellow's *The Adventures of Augie March,* but didn't like it. "But when I'm working," he said, "and read to get away from it, I'm inclined to make bad judgments about other people's writing." He thought Bellow's very early book, *Dangling Man,* much better.

One of the post-war writers who had impressed him most was John Horne Burns, who wrote *The Gallery* and two other novels and then, in 1953, died in circumstances that suggested suicide. "There was a fellow who wrote a fine book and then a stinking book about a prep school, and then he just blew himself up," Hemingway mused, adding a gesture that seemed to ask, How do you explain such a thing? He stared at nothing, seeming tired and sad.

"You know," he said, "my father shot himself."

There was silence. It had frequently been said that Hemingway never cared to talk about his father's suicide.

"Do you think it took courage?" I asked.

Hemingway pursued his lips and shook his head. "No. It's everybody's right, but there's a certain amount of egotism in it and a certain disregard of others." He turned off that conversation by picking up a handful of books. "Here are a few things you might like to look at before you turn off the light." He held out *The Retreat,* by P. H. Newby, Max Perkins' selected letters, *The Jungle Is Neutral,* by Frederick S. Chapman, and Malcolm Cowley's *The Literary Situation.*

By seven the next morning a rabble of dogs yipped and yelped in the yard near the finca's small guesthouse. René had been to town and returned with the mail and newspapers. Hemingway, in a tattered robe and old slippers, was already half through the *Times.*

"Did you finish the Cowley book last night?" he asked. "Very good, I think. I never realized what a tough time writers have economically, if they have it as tough as Malcolm says they do."

He was reminded of his early days in Paris. "It never seemed like hardship to me. It was hard work, but it was fun. I was working, and I had a wife and kid to support. I remember, first I used to go to the market every morning and get the stuff for Bumby's [his first son, John] bottle. His mother had to have her sleep." Lest this should be taken as a criticism, he added, "That's characteristic, you know, of the very finest women. They need their sleep, and when they get it, they're wonderful."

Another part of the routine in the Paris days, to pick up eating money, was Hemingway's daily trip to a gymnasium to work as a sparring partner for fighters. The pay was two dollars an hour. "That was very good money then, and I didn't get marked up very much. I had one rule: never provoke a fighter. I tried not to get hit. They had plenty of guys they could knock around."

He reached for the mail, slit open one from a pile of fifteen letters. It was from a high school English teacher in Miami, Florida, who complained that her students rarely read good literature and relied for "knowledge" on the movies, television, and radio. To arouse their interest, she wrote, she told them about Hemingway's adventures and pressed them to read his writings. "Therefore, in a sense," she concluded, "you are the teacher in my tenth grade classroom. I thought you'd like to know it." Hemingway found the letter depressing: "Pretty bad if kids are spending all that time away from books."

The next fishing expedition was *even* better than the first—fewer fish, but two of them were small marlin, one about eighty pounds, the other eighty-five, that struck simultaneously and were boated, Hemingway's with dispatch, the second at a cost of amateurish sweat and agony that was the subject of as much merriment as congratulations. It was a more sprightly occasion, too, because Mary Hemingway was able to come along. A bright, generous, and energetic woman, Hemingway's fourth wife cared for him well, anticipated his moods and his desires, enjoyed and played bountiful hostess to his friends, diplomatically turned aside some of the most taxing demands on his time and generosity. More than that, she shared his love and the broad mixture of interests—books, good talk, traveling, fishing, shooting—that were central to Hemingway's life. His marriage to her was plainly the central and guiding personal relationship of his last fifteen years.

Hemingway gazed happily at the pair of marlin. "We're back in business," he said, and gave Mary a hug. "This calls for celebration," said Mary.

"Off to the Floridita," said Hemingway.

The Floridita was once one of those comfortably shoddy Havana saloons where the food was cheap and good and the drinking serious. By then, enjoying a prosperity that was due in no small part to its reputation as the place you could see and maybe even drink with Papa Hemingway, it had taken on a red-plush grandeur and even had a velvet cord to block off the dining room entrance. "It looks crummy now," Hemingway said, "but the drinking's as good as ever."

The Floridita played a special role in Hemingway's life. "My not living in the United States," he explained, "does not mean any separation from the tongue or even the country. Any time I come to the Floridita I see Americans from all over. It can even be closer to America in many ways than being in New York. You go there for a drink or two, and see everybody from everyplace. I live in Cuba because I love Cuba—that does not mean a dislike for anyplace else. And because here I get privacy when I write. If I want to see anyone, I just go into town, or the Air Force guys come out to the place, naval characters and all—guys I knew in the war. I used to have privacy in Key West, but then I had less and less when I was trying to work, and there were too many people around, so I'd come over here and work in the Ambos Mundos Hotel."

The Floridita's bar was crowded, but several customers obligingly slid away from one section that had been designated long before by the proprietor as "Papa's Corner." Smiles. "Hello, Papa." Handshakes all around. "Three *Papa Dobles,*" said Hemingway, and the barkeep hastened to manufacture three immense daiquiris according to a Floridita recipe that relies more on grapefruit juice than on lemon or lime juice. The *Papa Doble* was a heavy seller in those days at $1.25, and a bargain at that.

Two sailors off a U.S. aircraft carrier worked up nerve to approach the author and ask for an autograph. "I read all your books," said one of them.

"What about you?" Hemingway said to the other.

"I don't read much," the young sailor said.

"Get started," Hemingway said.

The Floridita's owner appeared, with embraces for the Hemingways and the news that he was installing a modern men's room. Hemingway noted sadly that all the good things were passing. "A wonderful old john back there," he said. "Makes you want to shout: Water closets of the world unite; you have nothing to lose but your chains."

There were some other chances in later years to talk with Hemingway, in Cuba and New York, and there were a few letters in between—from Finca Vigia or Spain or France, or from Peru, where he went to fish with the Hollywood crew that made the film of *The Old Man and the Sea.* "Here's the chiropractor who fixed up my back," said the inscription on a postcard-size photograph from Peru showing him and an immense marlin he landed off Puerto Blanco.

Trips to New York grew less frequent and did not seem to amuse or entertain him. Unlike the old days and nights at Shor's or Twenty-one, he later usually preferred to see a few friends and dine in his hotel suite. Top health never really seemed to come back to him. He was having trouble with his weight, blood pressure, and diet. He was still working, though, as the stylishly written pages of *A Moveable Feast* show. (How much else he was producing then is not clear. Mrs. Hemingway, together with Scribner's and Hemingway's authorized biographer, Carlos Baker, and his old friend Malcolm Cowley, is sifting a trunkload of manuscripts that include some short stories, several poems, some fragments of novels, and at least one long completed novel about the sea—written to be part of a trilogy about land, sea, and air.)

His curiosity about the world, about people, about the old haunts (that word probably ought to be taken both ways) remained zestful, and so did his willingness to talk books and authors.

Once NBC did an hour-long radio documentary featuring recollections by many people who knew Hemingway, including some who were no longer friends. Sidney Franklin's comments annoyed him. "I never traveled with Franklin's bullfighting 'troupe,' " Hemingway said. "That is all ballroom bananas. I did pay for one of his operations, though, and tried to get him fights in Madrid when no promoter would have him, and staked him to cash so he wouldn't have to pawn his fighting suits." Max Eastman had retold on the broadcast his version of the memorable fight between him and Hemingway at Scribner's over Eastman's reflections on whether Hemingway really had any hair on his chest. "He was sort of comic," said Hemingway. "There used to be a character had a monologue something like Listen to What I Done to Philadelphia Jack O'Brien. Eastman is weakening though. In the original version he stood me on my head in a corner, and I screamed in a high-pitched voice."

Hemingway added: "None of this is of the slightest importance, and I never blow the whistle on anyone, nor dial N for Narcotics if I find a friend or enemy nursing the pipe."

On a later occasion, a dean of theology wrote in the *New Republic* an article entitled "The Mystique of Merde" about those he considered to be "dirty" writers, and put Hemingway near the top of his list. A newsmagazine reprinted part of the article, and when he read it, Hemingway, then in Spain, addressed as a rebuttal to the dean a hilarious short lecture on the true meaning of the word *merde* and its use as a word of honor among the military and theatrical people. It is, Hemingway explained, what all French officers say to one another when going on an especially dangerous mission or to their deaths, instead of *au revoir*, good-bye, good luck old boy, or any similar wet phrases. "I use old and bad words when they are necessary, but that does not make me a dirty writer," he said. For the dean, he had a dirty word. But he did not send the note to him; the writing of it turned his irritation into a shrug.

The Hemingways left Cuba in July of 1960 and went to Key West. From there, with luggage that filled a train compartment, they went to New York to live for a while in a small apartment. Later they moved to the new place Hemingway had bought in Ketchum, Idaho, close to the kind of shooting, fishing, walking that had beguiled him as a young boy in upper Michigan. He went to Spain for six weeks that summer to follow his friend Ordoñez and his rival, Dominguin, in their *mano a mano* tour of bullfights and to write *The Dangerous Summer,* bullfight pieces commissioned by *Life* magazine. I have the impression that he didn't think very much of them, but he didn't say. His spirits seemed low after that and ostensibly stayed that way, though he apparently kept at work out in Ketchum almost until the day his gun went off.

The rereading of the notes and letters from which these glimpses of Hemingway are drawn—for glimpses are all they are—induces a curious thought: It is possible that to have known him, at least to have known him superficially and late in his life, makes it more rather than less difficult to understand him.

He made himself easy to parody, but he was impossible to imitate. He sometimes did or said things that seemed almost perversely calculated to obscure his many gallantries and generosities and the many enjoyments and enthusiams he made possible for others. He could be fierce in his sensitivity to criticism and competitive in his craft to the point of vindictiveness, but he could laugh at himself ("I'm Ernie Hemorrhoid, the poor man's Pyle," he announced when he put on his war correspondent's uniform) and could enjoy the pure pride of believing that he had accomplished much of what he set out to do forty-five years before in a Parisian loft.

The private Hemingway was an artist. The public Hemingway was an experience, one from which small, sharp remembrances linger as persistently as the gusty moments:

A quiet dinner in New York when he remarked out of a rueful silence, and with a hint of surprise, "You know—all the beautiful women I know are growing old."

A misty afternoon in Cuba when he said, "If I could be something else, I'd like to be a painter."

A letter from the clinic in Rochester, Minnesota, where doctors were working him over: he reported "everything working o.k."—the blood pressure down from 250/125 to 130/80, and the weight down to 175 pounds, low for that big frame. He was two months behind, he said, on a book that was supposed to come out that fall—the fall of 1961.

And last of all, a Christmas card with the extra message in his climbing script: "We had fun, didn't we?"

Appendixes

Fascism Is a Lie

Ernest Hemingway/1937

Speech to the American Writers' Congress, New York, 4 June 1937.

A writer's problem does not change. He himself changes, but his problem remains the same. It is always how to write truly and, having found what is true, to project it in such a way that it becomes a part of the experience of the person who reads it.

There is nothing more difficult to do, and because of the difficulty, the rewards, whether they come early or late, are usually very great. If the rewards come early, the writer is often ruined by them. If they come too late, he is probably embittered. Sometimes they only come after he is dead, and then they cannot bother him. But because of the difficulty of making true, lasting writing, a really good writer is always sure of eventual recognition. Only romantics think that there are such things as unknown masters.

Really good writers are always rewarded under almost any existing system of government that they can tolerate. There is only one form of government that cannot produce good writers, and that system is fascism. For fascism is a lie told by bullies. A writer who will not lie cannot live or work under fascism.

Because fascism is a lie, it is condemned to literary sterility. And when it is past, it will have no history except the bloody history of murder that is well known and that a few of us have seen with our own eyes in the last few months.

A writer, when he knows what it is about and how it is done, grows accustomed to war. That is a serious truth which you discover. It is a shock to discover how truly used to it you become. When you are at the front each day and see trench warfare, open warfare, attacks, and counter-attacks, it all makes sense no matter what the cost in dead and wounded—when you know what the men are fighting for and that they are fighting intelligently. When men fight for the freedom of their country against a foreign invasion, and when these men are your friends—some new friends and some of long standing—and you know how they were attacked and how they fought, at first almost unarmed, you learn, watching them live and fight and die, that there are worse things than war. Cowardice is worse, treachery is worse, and simple selfishness is worse.

In Madrid, where it costs every British newspaper £57 or say $280 a week to insure a correspondent's life, and where the American correspondents work at an average wage of $65 a week uninsured, we of the working press watched murder done last month for nineteen days. It was done by German artillery, and it was highly efficient murder.

I said you grow accustomed to war. If you are interested enough in the science of it—and it is a great science—and in the problem of human conduct under danger, you can become so encompassed in it that it seems a nasty sort of egotism even to consider one's own fate. But no one becomes accustomed to murder. And murder on a large scale we saw every day for nineteen days during the last bombardments of Madrid.

The totalitarian fascist states believe in the totalitarian war. That, put simply, means that whenever they are beaten by armed forces they take their revenge on unarmed civilians. In this war, since the middle of November, they have been beaten at the Parque del Oeste, they have been beaten at the Pardo, they have been beaten at Carabanchel, they have been beaten on the Jarama, they have been beaten at Brihuega, and at Cordoba, and they are being fought to a standstill at Bilbao. Every time they are beaten in the field, they salvage that strange thing they call their honor by murdering civilians.

You have seen this murder in Joris Ivens's film, so I will not describe it. If I described it, it would only make you vomit. It might make you hate. But we do not want hate. We want a reasoned understanding of the criminality of fascism and how it should be opposed. We must realize that these murders are the gestures of a bully, the great bully of fascism. There is only one way to quell a bully, and that is to thrash him; and the bully of fascism is being beaten now in Spain as Napoleon was beaten in that same peninsula a hundred and thirty years ago. The fascist countries know it and are desperate. Italy knows her troops will not fight outside of Italy, nor, in spite of marvelous material, are they the equal as soldiers of the new Spanish regiments. There is no question of them ever equaling the fighters of the international brigades.

Germany has found that she cannot depend on Italy as an ally in any sort of offensive war. I have read that von Blomberg witnessed an impressive series of maneuvers yesterday with Marshal Badoglio, but it is one thing to maneuver on the Venetian plain with no enemy present, and another to be out-maneuvered and have three divisions destroyed on the plateau between Brihuega and Trijueja, by the Eleventh and Twelfth International Brigades and the fine Spanish troops of Lister, "Campesino," and Mera. It is one thing to bombard Almeria and take an undefended Málaga given up by treachery, and another to lose seven thousand troops before Cordoba and thirty thousand in unsuccessful assaults on Madrid. It is one thing to destroy Guernica and another to fail to take Bilbao.

I have talked too long. I started to speak of the difficulty of trying to write well and truly, and of the inevitable reward to those who achieve it. But in a time of war—and we are now in a time of war, whether we like it or not—the rewards are all suspended. It is very dangerous to write the truth in war, and the truth is also very dangerous to come by. I do not know just which American writers have gone out to seek it. I know many men of the Lincoln Battalion. But they are not writers. They are letter writers. Many British writers have gone. Many German writers have gone. Many French, and Dutch writers have gone; and when a man goes to seek the truth in war he may find death instead. But if twelve go and only two come back, the truth they bring will be the truth, and not the garbled hearsay that we pass as history. Whether the truth is worth some risk to come by, the writers must decide themselves. Certainly it is more comfortable to spend their time disputing learnedly on points of doctrine. And there will always be new schisms and new fallings-off and marvelous exotic doctrines and romantic lost leaders, for those who do not want to work at what they profess to believe in, but only to discuss and to maintain positions—skillfully chosen positions with no risk involved in holding them, positions to be held by the typewriter and consolidated with the fountain pen. But there is now, and there will be from now on for a long time, war for any writer to go to who wants to study it. It looks as though we are in for many years of undeclared wars. There are many ways that writers can go to them. Afterward there may be rewards. But that need not bother the writer's conscience. Because the rewards will not come for a long time. And he must not worry about them too much. Because if he is like Ralph Fox and some others he will not be there to receive them.

Nobel Prize Acceptance Speech

Read for Ernest Hemingway by John C. Cabot, United States
Ambassador to Sweden/10 December 1954

Members of the Swedish Academy, Ladies and Gentlemen:

Having no facility for speech-making and no command of oratory nor any domination of rhetoric, I wish to thank the administrators of the generosity of Alfred Nobel for this prize.

No writer who knows the great writers who did not receive the prize can accept it other than with humility. There is no need to list these writers. Everyone here may make his own list according to his knowledge and his conscience.

It would be impossible for me to ask the Ambassador of my country to read a speech in which a writer said all of the things which are in his heart. Things may not be immediately discernible in what a man writes, and in this sometimes he is fortunate; but eventually they are quite clear and by these and the degree of alchemy that he possesses he will endure or be forgotten.

Writing, at its best, is a lonely life. Organizations for writers palliate the writer's loneliness but I doubt if they improve his writing. He grows in public stature as he sheds his loneliness and often his work deteriorates. For he does his work alone and if he is a good enough writer he must face eternity, or the lack of it, each day.

For a true writer each book should be a new beginning where he tries again for something that is beyond attainment. He should always try for something that has never been done or that others have tried and failed. Then sometimes, with great luck, he will succeed.

How simple the writing of literature would be if it were only necessary to write in another way what has been well written. It is because we have had such great writers in the past that a writer is driven far out past where he can go, out to where no one can help him.

I have spoken too long for a writer. A writer should write what he has to say and not speak it. Again I thank you.

Index

199

DATE DUE